ALL WITH
SMILING FACES

ALL WITH SMILING FACES

PAUL BROWN

Goal-Post ▌▐

Published in 2014 by Goal-Post
An imprint of Superelastic
County Durham, UK
www.superelastic.co.uk

ISBN-13: 9780956227089

A CIP data record for this book is available from the
British Library

Cover painting by Paine Proffitt

For more information visit
www.allwithsmilingfaces.co.uk

'Oh me lads,
Ye should o' seen us gannin',
We pass'd the foaks upon the road,
Just as they wor stannin',
Thor wes lots o' lads an' lasses there,
All wi' smiling faces,
Gannin' alang the Scotswood Road,
To see the Blaydon Races.'

Blaydon Races
Geordie Ridley, 1862

Contents

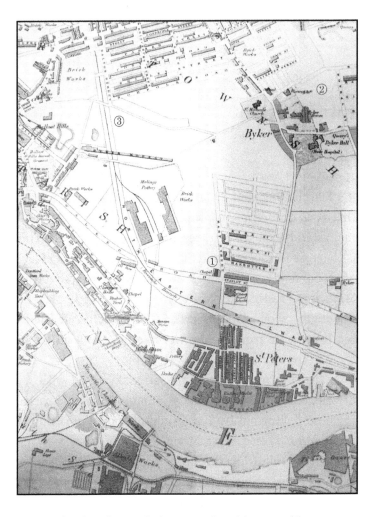

Map of Byker (c.1878) showing the old ground locations
of Newcastle United, formerly Stanley FC and East End:
1. Stanley Street, 2. The Vicarage/Bothal St, 3. Dalton St

Introduction

It's March 1987, and St James' Park is a football ground that's yet to become a proper stadium, with a decrepit main stand, exposed terraces, and brick wall urinals. This is the post-Heysel era, and fans are penned behind chicken coop fences. Hoardings around the pitch advertise Minories, Presto and Northern Rock. A single skeletal floodlight pylon cranes overhead. The smell of fermenting Brown Ale from the brewery across the road hangs thick in the air.

The afternoon is raw, the grey sky filled with icy drizzle, and I'm wrapped up in a much-worn blue parka, my nose poking out from the snorkel hood. I'm sitting in the timber-framed West Stand, condemned and facing demolition following the Bradford fire disaster. This is my first Newcastle United match, a birthday treat, in the 'posh seats' with my Uncle Terry. I've reached a malleable age at which I'm ready to be moulded and shaped by whatever the world has to throw at me. And the world has gone and chucked NUFC.

I was already a Newcastle fan long before I'd ever gone to a match, following the team's progress on Metro

Radio, in the *Football Pink*, and through very occasional live TV games. (I remember watching a woeful Newcastle team uncharacteristically thrash West Ham 4-0 on ITV's *The Big Match* earlier in the season, with Brian Moore commentating.)

I collected and read from cover to cover programmes from matches I'd never been to, and spent pocket money on scarves and badges from the old ladies at the supporters' club shop, located in a little prefab on Prudhoe Place. I got a Newcastle shirt for Christmas, a V-neck Umbro with broad black and white stripes, and a Newcastle Breweries blue star on the front. When the club sponsor changed, I got a Greenall's Beer logo patch from Prudhoe Place, and my mam sewed it over the star for me.

In following Newcastle I could hardly have been accused of being a glory seeker. Back in March '87 the club was rock bottom of the old first division, having won only five out of 28 league matches. Today's opponents Aston Villa had won only six. As sporting spectacles went, this was hardly Ali versus Frazier. Yet I was hopelessly excited. I can still remember the match, perhaps not as clearly as if it were yesterday, but certainly as if I'd quite recently re-watched it on YouTube.

I'm looking down on a mud-clodden pitch, markings embedded into the green-grey grass, nets draped from hooped goal-posts, referee holding a bright white ball, players wearing all-black boots. Then the game begins. The trill of the ref's whistle, the thump of boot against ball, the waxing and waning chatter and cheer of the crowd. And it's the crowd around me that really makes an impression. The atmosphere is as thick and as palpable as the brewery's fug. And then, as it happens, the match turns out to be pretty good, too.

Newcastle score first, through Tony Cunningham, who stretches his long legs to beat Villa's offside trap, then pokes the ball past keeper Nigel Spink. There's a rush of noise, and arms are raised towards the late-winter sky. '*Get in!*' Around me, seats clatter and folk stamp their feet, causing the stand's wooden floorboards to bounce and creak. Below, the Gallowgate-enders sway back and forth as if caught in a swelling tide. But Villa equalise, and the thin sound of a few hundred away fans is surrounded by a gloomy silence. At half-time, the big electronic scoreboard reads '1-1'.

Then Peter Beardsley cuts in from the left flank, swivelling his hips like an Elvis impersonator. He quick-steps, and quick-steps again, reaches the edge of the area, twists those hips, then *bang*. A right-foot shot, straight as a draftsman's rule, buried in the bottom-left corner. The goal celebrations have an extra thrust – the noise is louder, the arms are higher, the old stand bounces and shakes even more precariously. It's not just a goal, and not just a winning goal. It's a moment of magic, and a communal moment, shared with a gang I already know I want to stay a part of.

Football's not just about winning, and never has been for me (which is fortunate considering Newcastle's inability to win anything during my lifetime). It's about those shared moments that make your chest pound and your stomach swirl. Or perhaps that was the half-time pie. In any case, Newcastle won my first match 2-1, and then somehow managed to avoid relegation. I started going to every game, and never stopped. Gut me, fillet me and stick me on the grill – I was completely hooked.

But the thing is, it was always going to be this way. I could not have been anything other than a Newcastle United supporter. I grew up within sight of the Tyne, and everyone I knew supported Newcastle. I didn't have a choice, it just happened. Some football fans pick their team based on favourite players, or on strip colours, or on who won the FA Cup in a particularly formative year. But for a lot of us it simply comes down to where you were born and grew up, and who your family support. I was a Newcastle supporter, and that's just the way it was. No complaints here.

Is Newcastle United in my blood? I don't know, I'd have to ask a phlebotomist. But it certainly feels like I was predestined to be a Newcastle supporter. Many of us can trace the lineage of our support through family trees, via our parents, our grandparents and so on. But Newcastle United has only been around since 1881, so that lineage of support can only stretch back a few generations. At some point one of our recent ancestors decided, consciously or otherwise, to become a Newcastle supporter. They could never have known how that decision would affect future generations. But it can all be traced back to them. It's all their fault.

My own NUFC lineage goes back beyond the memories of any living relatives, so I can't say for sure when my family's support for Newcastle United began. There are no Edwardian season tickets in shoe boxes, and no Victorian share certificates in lofts, no stories of away trips by horse and carriage passed down through the generations. The only clue I have is a torn and crumbling photograph.

The photo is of my great-grandad, Richardson Robson Flinn. It was taken during the First World War, and he's pictured wearing a football kit in a group shot of what looks to be his battalion team. The top of the photo is missing, slicing off the heads of several of his teammates. Richardson kneels front and centre, wearing a football shirt that is tied at his neck with laces. Someone, a well-meaning relative, has drawn a circle around his head.

Richardson was shot and gassed during the war and, although he survived and made it home, he never properly recovered, and he died at a relatively young age. There's no-one left around who knew him. So I can't say for sure how keen his attachment was to Newcastle United. But he obviously played football, and he grew up in the same place as me, overlooking the Tyne, almost close enough to hear the roar of the St James' Park crowd. Surely he must have been drawn towards the Magpies during their greatest golden era.

He was born in 1892, in the year that the club changed its name from East End to Newcastle United, and he grew up as the club was growing, through the Northern League, into the Football League, up to the first division, where they became League champions three times in five years. He was 18 years old in April 1910, when Newcastle won the FA Cup. It was a huge and historic achievement, one that was embraced and celebrated by virtually the whole of Tyneside, so it's difficult to believe he wouldn't have been affected by it. If he wasn't already a Newcastle United fan (perhaps following a lineage that stretched back via his father, and grandfather) then surely the triumphs of the Edwardian champions must have sealed the deal.

So this book is for Richardson Robson, and all our other ancestors, recent and far-removed, who have passed down their support for Newcastle United, a big, beautiful football club with equal power to delight and frustrate, but without which our lives would be a lot less interesting. The book is an attempt to find out how it all started – how the club was formed, how it became successful, and how it came to mean so much to so many of us. It's an attempt to find out what made Newcastle United so special, and to find out what made it 'wor club'.

Paul Brown, 2014
- A Faithful Son of Father Tyne

The author's great-grandfather, front row centre, c.1914

*'Newcastle-upon-Tyne' wood print engraved by R Paterson
from a painting by J O'Connor, the Art Journal, 1882*

*Location of the Stanley Street ground, 'near Stanley Street',
now Walker Road, at Raby Street, Byker (photo Paul J White)*

1

Stanley Street

This is where it all started for Newcastle United – in a car park behind a tile warehouse a couple of miles east of St James' Park. It wasn't a car park back in 1881, of course, and nothing remains to mark the fact that one of football's biggest clubs played its first ever match here.

A few cars are spaced around the parking bays under a big red sign that says 'Tile Sale'. Next to the cars is a triangle of grass with a green commercial wheelie bin in the middle, and four gangly trees arranged – if you use your imagination – like two sets of goalposts. A few yards away, lorries rattle along Walker Road, which runs from the eastern edge of Newcastle city centre along the north bank of the River Tyne.

Back in the 1880s this particular stretch of Walker Road, in the Byker district of Newcastle, was known as Stanley Street. It was a workers' terrace – a modest row of red-brick houses, butted up against each other along a cobbled road, with billowing chimney stacks on the roofs, and outdoor toilets (or netties) in the yards. This part of South Byker, near to St Peter's, was a rapidly-developing residential area, with grids of houses spilling down the riverbank towards the thriving industries of the Tyne.

Newcastle was enjoying a golden age as a power-house of industry. The town (it would gain city status in 1882) was prospering due to its expertise in shipbuilding and other heavy industries. The river was alive with activity, packed with tugs, barges and dredgers, tall-masted sailing ships, rattling propeller boats, and billow-ing steamers. Its banks were lined with an unbroken chain of engineering works, coal staiths and shipbuilding yards, cement works, iron foundries and grain ware-houses.

Many of the residents of Stanley Street worked at the quayside, in the shipyards, or on the river itself. All things considered, Stanley Street was a pretty average working class terrace. And it was here, in November 1881, that a group of pretty average working class lads played their first match as Stanley FC – the club that would become Newcastle United.

I've come here to get a feel for the early days of the club, for the players and the supporters who were here at the beginning, before Shearer, Milburn and Gallacher, before St James' Park, the Toon Army and the black and white stripes. Some history books and internet sites will tell you that Newcastle United formed in 1892, and it's true that's when the club adopted the name and moved to St James'. But before that they were East End, and before that they were Stanley FC. And this tile warehouse car park represents the location of the football field where hundreds of thousands of black and white dreams began.

The football club that began as Stanley FC was

formed to give the players of Stanley Cricket Club something to do in the winter months. Cricket had been popular for decades, but football was still an emerging game. The Football Association had formed in 1863, but the rules were still being debated and developed. Football was still closely tied to the public schools, and was dominated by teams such as Wanderers, Oxford University and Old Etonians. The 1881 FA Cup final was won by Old Carthusians – the old boys' team of Charterhouse School. But the public schools' grip on the game was coming to an end. Football was blossoming in 'the provinces', and working class towns such as Sheffield, Glasgow and Blackburn were becoming hubs of the game. Football was about to experience a popular revolution, and Newcastle was ready to join in.

Standing here today, it seems almost impossible that this city could have once existed without football. The game and the place are now so closely entwined that they seem to share a heartbeat. The pulse of the city ebbs and wanes in sympathy with the fortunes of Newcastle United. Defeat darkens the mood like the blackest thundercloud. Life weighs more heavily on the shoulders. Victory seems as rare as warm sunshine, but when it comes the city basks in it. After a weekend win, Monday morning commuters can share a smile. Visitors searching for football need not even raise their eyes to the city's skyline and the great cathedral of St James' Park. Newcastle's obsession is so conspicuous that it can almost be tasted and touched. Football is as thick in the air as the fog on the Tyne.

Football has probably been played in Newcastle in

one form or another since the Romans first settled on the banks of this big river back in the 2nd century. The Romans played a ball game called harpastum, a violent affair that seems to have been a kind of ultimate fighting version of rugby. By medieval times, this had morphed into the only slightly more civilised 'mob football' game, played between hundreds of villagers and townsfolk, usually on public holidays, particularly Shrove Tuesday. You often see 'Shrovetide football' turning up on regional news broadcasts, as it's still traditionally played in villages and towns today, notably in Alnwick in Northumberland and Sedgefield in County Durham.

Records suggest that the first club formed with the intention of playing football in Newcastle was the Early Risers, which existed from at least 1848. Members met on the Town Moor at six o'clock every morning to play football, cricket and quoits, and afterwards ate breakfast together 'with an appetite of 40 ploughman-power'. The Victorian equivalent of a visit to the gym followed by a McMuffin, I suppose. This was long before the formation of the FA and the creation of Laws of the Game, and football was still just a casual recreational pursuit – a world away from the all-encompassing behemoth it would later become.

Association football didn't really arrive in Newcastle until the late 1870s, as newly-educated young gentlemen returned home from their public schools and universities, and disparate groups of working men were drawn to the region's then-prosperous industries. They brought with them leather boots, ox-bladder balls, and pamphlets explaining the Laws of the Game, and they told tales of great matches played and witnessed in far-flung parts of the country. Now they wanted to play the game here, so they set up Newcastle's first association football clubs – Tyne (sometimes referred to as Tyne Association) and Rangers.

Tyne was formed in 1877 with the specific intention of popularising football in the local area. With this pioneering intention, the club was following in the footsteps of the likes of Sheffield FC, Queen's Park in Glasgow, and Forest FC (later renamed Wanderers) in North London. The club's trial match, at Elswick Rugby Club on 3 March 1877, was one of the first games ever played on Tyneside under association rules. Tyne's home ground was at Eskdale Terrace in Jesmond, to the north of Newcastle city centre, now the location of the Royal Grammar School.

Rangers was formed a year after Tyne, and initially played on the other side of the river, in Gateshead, at the Drill Field on Prince Consort Road. They moved back to Newcastle in 1880, claiming a ground on the Castle Leazes area of the Town Moor that would soon become known as St James' Park. You might have heard of it.

The football played by these two pioneer clubs was pretty distinct from the modern game. It was rudimentary and rough, with unfamiliar rules and copious injuries. There was little room for tactics or finesse, and passing and teamwork had yet to be embraced. Most sides lined up with at least six forwards, but, despite the emphasis on forward play, goals were hard to come by. Burly defenders would barge opponents to the floor, and muddy scrimmages would ensue, with the heavy leather ball going nowhere very fast. It was a game that divided opinion. Some newspaper correspondents complained that football was primitive and dangerous, but others thought it was a whole lot of fun.

Writing in the *Newcastle Courant* newspaper, a Victorian correspondent identified only as JD wrote of his attempt to convince a friend of the merits of football. 'Despite my friend's candid opinions and his own bad terms with it, I must confess that I have myself a strong predilection for football,' he wrote. 'It brings into play all the wits of a man's mind and every sinew of his body, so that it is at once wholesome and invigorating to both.'

Tyne and Rangers soon established themselves among the leading football clubs of the North East, alongside the likes of Middlesbrough (formed in 1876) and Sunderland (1879). Although both Tyne and Rangers had public school roots, they became clubs of their communities, recruiting players and attracting spectators from a broad section of local society. Their prominence helped generate interest in the game and encourage the formation of other local clubs, including North Eastern (a works team of the North Eastern Railway Company) and Elswick Leather Works.

Proof of football's growing popularity came in January 1880, when a specially-assembled Newcastle and District team (billed, interestingly, as 'Tyne United') faced a touring Scottish FA side (dubbed the 'Scotch Canadians' due to the fact they were playing to raise money to visit Canada). 2,000 spectators turned up to watch the match – by far the biggest that had ever been played in Newcastle. The crowd was likely quite diverse, encompassing gentlemen associated with Tyne and Rangers, and working men who had read about famous Scottish players such as Tom Vallance and George Ker in their newspapers. Bowler hats mixed with flat caps, as football united the town. The local team lost 5-0, but the result was pretty much immaterial. Newcastle had caught the football bug.

Did any of the lads from Stanley Street attend the 'Tyne United' match? It's possible, and the visit of the 'Scotch Canadians' could easily have inspired a few kick-abouts along the terraced back lanes just across the way from where I'm standing. Back in 1881 there was a boarding school here, and a chapel at the end of the terrace. The back lanes are gone now, as are the school and chapel. The Stanley Street site is covered by grass and a row of trees. Where the chapel once stood is St Peter's Social Club, a red brick building with an intriguing sign over the doorway depicting a knight standing over the industrial Tyne. Next to the social club is the tile warehouse, and behind that is the car park that pretty much represents the location of Stanley FC's pitch.

It's difficult to pinpoint the precise location. The records say only that the club 'played on vacant land near Stanley Street in South Byker'. Old maps show there was a large open area – with room for about six football pitches – between the chapel and the famous Maling Pottery. The pottery, once claimed to be the largest in the world, was built in 1879, a couple of years before Stanley FC came into existence, and several Stanley Street residents worked there. It closed in 1963, but some of the original buildings still stand, including the tall clocktower, in the estate now known as Hoult's Yard. If we can build a picture of what Stanley's pitch might have looked like, that clocktower would be visible in the background.

There's a bloke standing outside the social club sucking on a cigarette and no doubt wondering why someone is taking such an interest in a seemingly uninspiring car park. The social club and tile warehouse pretty much obscure any view of the river from my vantage point. In 1881, players standing on Stanley's pitch would have been able to see all the way down to the Tyne, and survey all of the bustling industries that lined its banks. There would have been something of a whiff in the air. The Tyne itself was pretty much an open sewer, so full of effluent and debris that constant dredging was required to keep it open for shipping. Then there were brick works, manure works and other factories belching out dust and smoke, plus a huge chemical works on the other side of the river. Not, you would think, the ideal environment for a stroll around a football pitch.

And then there was the slope. St James' Park has a noticeably sloping pitch to this day, but the Stanley Street pitch must have been much worse, sitting partway down the fairly steep bank that leads from Byker to the river. One early match report does make reference to the slope, highlighting the difficulties teams faced when playing against it. It's steep enough that if you were to have a kick-about on the car park today and the ball rolled into the street, you'd have to make a pretty sharp dash to make sure you didn't lose it as it spun its way down towards the Tyne.

Stanley FC's first captain – and by extension the first captain of Newcastle United – lived just around the corner from the Stanley pitch, at number 12 Raby Street. William Coulson was just 18 years old when the club was formed, and was working as an assistant teacher at a local school. According to the 1881 census, he was the eldest of six children of John and Mary Coulson. John was a joiner, unemployed at the time of the census, and Mary was a housewife. William's 13-year-old brother Robert worked as an errand boy, but the other children – two boys and two girls – were too young to work. So William was the main breadwinner for his family – an assistant teacher's salary to feed eight mouths. He probably earned less than a pound a week – the equivalent of around £50 today.

William was the captain and opening batsman for the Stanley cricket team. He would have been present at a meeting of the cricket club, held at the house of a Mr Allan on Shields Road in Byker in November 1881, during which the formation of a football club was discussed. Despite his youth he must have been a mature lad whose leadership qualities were recognised by his peers. His role as captain would have involved picking the football team, many of them fellow cricketers, all of them young lads from the surrounding streets, with most of them coming down the bank from the more densely-populated areas of North Byker and Heaton.

Half-back John 'Chippy' Armstrong was 18, a ship's joiner who lived on Harbottle Street, across the road from the Stanley pitch. Forwards William and Robert Findlay (or Finlay) were brothers, aged 17 and 15. Born in

Scotland, they now lived on Belvedere Street, just off Shields Road in Byker, and both worked as clerks. John Dixon and George McKenzie were both 18, both forwards, and both clerks living in Byker. John Cook, another forward and another clerk, lived just north of Shields Road, in Heaton, on South View West. Then there was Thomas Phalp, the 19-year-old goalkeeper, who worked as a clerk and lived on Heaton Terrace. Full-back John Hobson was the youngest player in the team at just 14 years of age. He lived on West View and worked as a plumber.

What's remarkable here from a trawl through the census is the revelation that this football club was formed by a bunch of teenagers, the oldest of whom was only 19. A group of young lads forming a football team with their mates – it's something that still happens in communities all over the world to this day. Teams come together, time passes, interest dwindles, mates drift away, teams fold. But this team, formed here in November 1881, was different. As they kicked a ball about on the pitch in South Byker, these lads could have had no inkling whatsoever of what they had started.

And the club got off to a flying start. The first match was played on 26 November 1881 at Stanley Street against invited guests the Elswick Leather Works 'Reservers'. George McKenzie scored Stanley's (and therefore Newcastle United's) first ever goal in a 5-0 win. John Dixon scored twice, and William Coulson and William Findlay scored, too. Stanley's formation was typically attack-minded for the era – they lined up 2-2-6. The short-lived *Tyneside Daily Echo* newspaper printed a brief summary of 'a pleasant game', likely filed by William

Findlay, who was the club secretary. 'The first half was of a give and take description, but in the second half the Stanley team had the wind in their favour,' the report explained.

The report doesn't reveal what the teams wore. Football kit was expensive, and it's quite possible that the Stanley players followed the lead of players from other fledgling clubs and turned out in their cricket whites, or whatever jumble of sports clothes they could get their hands on. The pitch would have looked strange to modern spectators. It's unlikely that there would have been any pitch markings, and instead the boundary may have been cordoned off with rope. Goal nets had yet to be introduced, and tape would have been strung between the goalposts instead of solid crossbars. The rules were different, too. With no penalty area to constrain him, the goalkeeper could handle the ball wherever he liked, and there were no penalty kicks. There would not necessarily have been a referee to keep order. As captain, William Coulson would have been relied upon to implement the rules and settle disputes.

Understandably, there's no record of an attendance figure for Stanley's first match. Like most early football clubs, this was a recreation club formed for its members to play football, with no real expectation that anyone would watch them. The first spectators were non-playing members, so we can imagine a few friends stood along the touch-line, some cricketers taking in this new spectacle, and perhaps a handful of curious spectators from Byker. Maybe a few residents of Stanley Street, drawn by the yells and thuds of leather on leather, stuck a head out of a window, or wandered across the road to watch Stanley's first game, effectively becoming founding members of the Toon Army.

Football was only just becoming a spectator sport. 4,000 had attended the 1881 FA Cup final, and clubs were starting to generate profits through gate receipts. But the crowd at the first ever match of the club that became Newcastle United was substantially smaller than the 52,000 we're used to today. 52 without the thousand might be a pretty good estimate. Still, though, what a milestone of an event this would be to go back in time and witness. Any Newcastle fan who happens to somehow gain possession of their own personal time machine should eschew popular history and instead set the controls for Byker in November 1881.

Although Stanley FC was by no means the first football club on Tyneside, it was one of the first to have been formed by working folk from the area. While Tyne and Rangers had done much to help popularise the game on Tyneside, they were clubs that were primarily formed by public school old boys. The match between Stanley and the Elswick Leather Works team was a proper proletarian affair, and this might have engaged local people more than previous matches would have. We know from census records that the residents of Stanley Street had diverse occupations, working as platers and riveters at the shipyards, steam tugmen on the river, potters at Maling, ropemakers, boilersmiths, and in one case a baker and confectioner.

Although booming industry provided plenty of jobs, life was pretty tough. Working hours were long, wages were low, and living conditions were poor. Most folk worked six days a week, and the average wage for a labourer was £30 per year. Without proper sanitation, the densely-populated streets were rife with disease. Byker was regarded as a 'fever den' in the 1880s, and epidemics of cholera, influenza and other illnesses swept from door to door taking hundreds of lives. The chance to play or watch football must have provided a welcome escape from the realities of life.

Because Stanley FC had been formed by members of a cricket club, it had a ready-made micro community of players and supporters to call upon. This helped the club survive in the face of competition from other – mostly short-lived – local clubs. Football clubs were popping up all over the place, but there wasn't enough widespread interest to sustain them all. Most would play a handful of matches and then disappear. Those that survived generally did so because they had some kind of established infrastructure behind them.

Many of modern football's biggest clubs were formed during the Victorian era from existing institutions such as cricket clubs, workplaces, schools and churches. Manchester United was formed by workers at a railway depot in Newton Heath, and Arsenal was formed by workers at the Royal Arsenal in Woolwich. Everton originated at St Domingo's Methodist Church, Manchester City was formed by the Rector of St Mark's Church, and Aston Villa was formed at the Villa Cross Wesleyan Chapel. Tottenham Hotspur was formed by boys at All Hallows Church. West Ham was a workers' team from the Thames Ironworks, and Sunderland AFC was originally

Sunderland and District Teachers AFC. Gradually, these clubs expanded beyond their institutions and began to represent their communities, town and cities.

Stanley seem to have had a pretty decent team. In order to have won their first ever match 5-0 against established opposition ('reservers' or otherwise), they must have had plenty of training – arranging practice matches amongst themselves, working out the rules, figuring out who could kick straight, and picking a first team. Records show Stanley won seven out of 11 games in the 1881/82 season. By the latter half of the season they were playing fairly regularly, home and away, against teams such as Derwent Rovers and Burnopfield. They also played against a reserve side from Rangers, and a Newcastle FA team, and beat both of them.

The Stanley club also operated a reserve side, made up of under-16s, including William Coulson's 13-year-old brother Robert, and 14-year-old Robert Lightfoot, who lived with his innkeeper dad John in the Cumberland Arms pub, which still stands today, just off Byker Bank, not far from the old Stanley Street. So Stanley FC had got off to a pretty good start. The club was well-organised and was winning games, and was starting to make an impression in the developing world of North East football. This was a club that was going places.

But the name of Stanley FC would soon be consigned to the history books. There had been some confusion involving the team from Stanley Street and teams from the town of Stanley in County Durham. Also, the name of the street they originated from was falling out of use, with Stanley Street increasingly being referred to as part of New Walker Road. Perhaps most importantly, there was news of another team that had just formed in the west of the city. This new team, based in Elswick, was to be called West End. So, in 1882, Stanley FC changed its name to East End.

The *Daily Echo*, reported the news in typically matter-of-fact style: 'At a meeting of the Stanley Association Football Club, Byker, held lately, it was resolved to change the name to the East End.'

The club played its first game as East End on 7 October 1882, beating Hamsterley Rangers 1-0. Across town on the same day, soon-to-be rivals West End played their first game, losing 2-0 to a team called Rosewood. The latter were from Byker, and within a few months they had been absorbed by upwardly-mobile neighbours East End. So East End gained several new players, but they also lost a few, including keeper Thomas Phalp, who left to join other clubs.

Up until this point, all of the club's matches had been friendlies, but East End ('late Stanley', as newspapers reminded) played their first competitive match on 13 January 1883 in the first round of the Northumberland and Durham FA Senior Cup. The match was played at Stanley Street, and the opponents were Elswick Leather Works – the first team rather than the 'reservers' this time. William Coulson captained East End, and John Armstrong and the Findlay brothers were also in the side. For the first time, we have an indication of the club's kit – navy blue jerseys and white knickerbockers (or baggy-kneed short pants). East End matched their visitors in the first half, and changed ends with the score at 1-1. But they conceded another goal after half-time, and eventually lost 2-1. East End's – and Newcastle United's – first ever competitive match had ended in defeat.

That was William Coulson's last game for the club. And it was one of the last games East End played at Stanley Street. At the end-of-season meeting in April 1883, at Mr Greenwell's Refreshment Rooms in Heaton, the club was reported to be in a 'flourishing state'. Although the first season under the name East End hadn't been particularly successful in terms of results, the club had achieved enough to feel secure in its future and optimistic of good times ahead. The players ate a 'sumptuous' supper, made speeches, and sang songs. They had successfully laid the foundations for a football club that would come to be bigger and more important than any of them could possibly imagine.

Back in the present day, the bloke outside the social club finishes his cigarette and heads inside. A delivery van pulls up outside the tile warehouse. The trees in the car park stand silent, never a ball rattled between them. Football is long gone from this place. East End had outgrown Stanley Street, so it's time for us to move on.

The club's next ground was located up the bank in Byker, requiring a walk up Raby Street, where William Coulson lived. During his time, this would have been a busy trading street, lined with shops supplying all manner of goods to the surrounding homes and businesses. You can imagine William sending his younger siblings out on errands to pick up provisions, handing them a few precious pennies with which to feed the family. There's nothing left of those bustling Victorian times, the entire area now completely redeveloped. His home is long gone, but what happened to William Coulson?

Having co-founded Stanley FC, and captained Stanley and East End, he was still only 20 years old when he played his last match for the club. He was presented with a gold pin to mark his role in the formation and development of the club. But why did he stop playing? It's possible that he was injured, perhaps in that cup defeat by Elswick, although records show he did continue to play for the East End cricket team. It's more likely that he, and several other founding members, simply found they weren't good enough to continue playing as the club increased in stature and faced more experienced opponents. Perhaps the club he founded outgrew him. Like many young footballers, perhaps he didn't quite make the grade.

Coulson did remain involved with East End for a few years, and briefly acted as club secretary. After that, as the club moved onwards and upwards, its founder seems to have drifted away. By the 1890s he was living with his wife Elizabeth in Rennington, near Alnwick in Northumberland, and working as headmaster of the village school.

Meanwhile, Newcastle United – the club he had helped create – grew into one of the biggest football clubs in the country. It seems fair to believe that the name of William Coulson should be better known among football fans of a black and white persuasion today.

Location of the Vicarage/Bothal Street ground, behind the Old Vicarage at the east end of the Byker Wall (photo Paul J White)

Location of the Dalton Street ground, at the west end of the Byker Wall, near Conyers Road, Byker (photo Paul J White)

2

Byker Boys

It's an unusual name, Byker, and there isn't another place on Earth that shares it. The name was bestowed by Viking invaders, and its Norse meaning is 'village by marshy woodland'. So we know that this has been a residential area since at least the ninth century, a millennium before football invaded the area.

Maps from the 1880s show that in East End's time Byker was experiencing rapid growth. Industry and housing were creeping up the river bank, with the brick works churning out materials to build more terraces, and street grids being marked out across the remaining open spaces. More industry meant more workers, and, within the space of a decade or so, this area grew into a bustling community.

Byker is probably most famous outside of the area as the fictional setting of *Byker Grove*, the BBC kids' drama that kick-started the careers of Geordie TV heroes Ant and Dec and, to an admittedly lesser extent, Spuggy. It's also well known for strikingly-unique housing development the Byker Wall, an award-winning grade II listed estate, which was built in the 1970s following the slum clearance that demolished the terraced houses that stood here during East End's time. The site East End moved to in 1883 is at the east end, appropriately enough, of the half-mile long Wall.

The journey up to the Wall brings us to a chapter in Newcastle United's history that contains the club's first genuinely great player and something that has been all too rare in modern times – silverware. The fact the club won trophies before changing its name to Newcastle United must surely be reason enough to explore its pre-1892 history.

In any case, claims from various sources (official and unofficial) that the club was formed in 1892 are disingenuous. Embracing the fact that it was formed in 1881 rather than 1892 brings Newcastle into line with other big clubs that were officially formed under different names. Newcastle United was formed in 1881 as Stanley FC, just as Manchester United was formed in 1878 as Newton Heath, and Arsenal was formed in 1886 as Dial Square. Whether Stanley or East End or Newcastle United, it's an unavoidable fact that the few handfuls of supporters the club had in the early 1880s enjoyed more success than the hundreds of thousands of supporters that follow the club today.

Those who did follow East End in 1883 would have had to make a short, steep walk up to the club's new ground, located about half a mile up the bank from the Stanley Street pitch, behind St Michael's Vicarage. St Michael's Church still stands inside the Byker Wall development, although it's in a state of disrepair, and the Vicarage itself has become a small block of flats, named

The Old Vicarage. The football pitch would have lain between the Vicarage and Bothal Street to the east.

There's some open grass here now, and a row of the Byker Wall's distinctive maisonettes. Following Old Vicarage Walk brings you to a set of gate posts that mark the boundary between the open space and the road. The posts are Victorian, but they were built after East End's time here, in 1889, at the entrance of the Victoria Jubilee School, which was demolished to make way for the building of the Byker Wall. This is a much flatter area than the Stanley Street location, although it's still on a hill, and it's nearer to the busier areas of North Byker and Heaton.

One notable match played at the Old Vicarage site was against Sunderland on 3 November 1883. This was effectively the first ever Newcastle United versus Sunderland Tyne-Wear derby match. With William Coulson no longer playing, William Findlay, the Scots-born Byker lad, took over the captaincy of the team. Regrettably for the Tynesiders, first spoils in the local derby went to Wearside, with Sunderland winning 3-0. Although this must have rankled, the result was not the disgrace it might be today. Sunderland was a more experienced club, a couple of years older than East End, with many more matches under its belt. The Newcastle club would have to endure a few more Tyne-Wear defeats before parity was achieved.

In the following week there was another important fixture – the first match between East End and cross-town rivals West End. The Findlay brothers and John Armstrong were in the East End team, while West End lined up with the Mather brothers, W and J, alongside influential club secretary Bill Tiffin. This early 'Newcastle derby' finished 1-1. There would be little to separate East End and West End over the next few years.

East End were improving as a team and growing as a club. And as it grew, costs increased. The club had to pay for ground maintenance, goal-posts, corner flags and leather balls. They needed kits for the first team and the reserves, and transport to away matches. These costs were initially covered by members' subscriptions, but as the club expanded it would have needed another revenue stream – and that would have come from paying spectators. The club became reliant on its fans.

The relocation to a more populated area and the pull of more attractive fixtures would have helped to increase East End's early attendances. Figures aren't recorded, but we're still only talking about a hundred or so spectators – perhaps not many more than a top Sunday League team might attract today. Even so, East End were looking for a more suitable ground, so they left the Vicarage and moved to another pitch about half a mile west – near the opposite end of what is now the Byker Wall.

To get there, we need to walk through the Wall estate, a labyrinth of paths, steps and tunnels that's pretty confusing to an outsider. Designed by Ralph Erskine, the Wall and its estate is a multi-coloured Lego box of interlinked homes. It's mostly pedestrianised, with car parks at the edges of the estate. The Wall itself was designed to protect the dwellings within from the noise and pollution caused by a planned adjacent motorway that in the end never became more than a dual-lane bypass.

East End's next ground was located at Dalton Street, next to the North Eastern Railway line. The line is still here, separated from Dalton Street by a stone wall. No doubt during East End's time here the odd heavy leather caser would have disappeared over that wall down onto the railway tracks below. The pitch had been vacated by the now-defunct Newcastle Rangers. East End snapped up a few of Rangers' best players, too. One of those players was a chap called Alec White, more of whom very soon. The location of the pitch would have been somewhere in the open space between what was Norfolk Road and the Byker Ropery, or today midway between Conyers Road and St Michael's Road.

Again, the pitch was on an incline, high above the river. This vantage point offers a distracting view over the Ouseburn Valley and down to the Tyne. In 1884, before high-rise developments, the view would have stretched all the way down to the High Level Bridge and the then relatively new Swing Bridge on Newcastle's Quayside. The famous Tyne Bridge, of course, wasn't built until the 1920s. The Byker Bridge, across the Ouseburn tributary of the Tyne, was opened as a toll bridge in 1878, and would have cost spectators travelling to watch East End half a penny to cross.

By this point we know from newspaper reports that East End were attracting crowds of two or three hundred spectators, so in modern terms we're up to non-league level, equivalent to decent attendances in the North East's Northern League. The club was generating income and making a profit, and although virtually nothing is recorded about the Dalton Street ground, we can assume that it would at least have been surrounded by some form of fencing to prevent spectators who weren't club members from watching without handing over a penny or so to the gateman. At a time when there were few recreation options available to the working class beyond going to the pub, it's easy to see how the club could have attracted a growing number of local folk.

On a broader level, football was emerging as a popular game of the people. Once the preserve of the public school elite, the game had been wrenched away by the working class. This social shift in the game is clearly visible if you take a look at a list of early FA Cup winners. From the competition's inception, the cup had only been won by southern-based old boys' clubs such as Wanderers and Oxford University. But in 1883 the cup was won by Blackburn Olympic – a northern team of factory workers and tradesmen. In 1884 it was won by the similarly working class Blackburn Rovers, who went on to win it three consecutive times. The old boys had lost their grip on the FA Cup – and on the game of football. It was now the game of the people, and the people of Newcastle took it to their hearts.

Going back to the comparison with modern non-league football, that might just help us to identify a little better with these early spectators. If you've ever been to a non-league match, in the Northern League or elsewhere, then you'll no doubt have noticed that almost every person there seems to be involved with the club in some way, whether they're taking gate money and selling programmes, pulling pints and serving pies, organising fundraisers and doing the books, or just offering first-name-basis encouragement from the sidelines. They're football supporters of the truest kind, because they're actually keeping the club going, helping it to survive. Whether they're committee members or just paying punters, they know the players, live in the same streets as them, drink in the same pubs as them.

If we could roll back to the early 1880s, we'd find something similar emerging around East End – a club run and represented by people from the local community. It must have been fairly easy for early spectators to establish a connection with the club – and to begin to support it. They were cheering on their friends and neighbours, who were representing their local community against rivals from across town or further afield. It would have seemed entirely alien to support anything other than your local team. East End FC belonged to the local community, and that connection remained as the club expanded and grew.

1884/85 was a pivotal season for East End. Now captained by John 'Chippy' Armstrong, and fuelled by the goals of former Newcastle Rangers players Teddy Hiscock and Tommy Hoban, the club established itself as a real force in North East football. But it was the arrival of another former Rangers player that really pushed East End forward. This was a tough Scot who pulled strings and scored goals from centre-half – which was then a central midfield position. He was a hugely important addition to the club, and his name was Alec White.

Although few football history books make room for him (and he doesn't even have a Wikipedia entry), there's no doubt White is one of the most influential characters in the history of Newcastle United Football Club. One book that does afford him a mention is the essential 1960 North East football tome *Hotbed of Soccer* by Arthur Appleton, who calls White, 'the outstanding figure in early East End history'. White was clearly an excellent player – perhaps the best local player of his generation – but was also an inspirational leader.

Alexander Henry White was born in the village of Airlie, near Glamis Castle in Angus, Scotland, in 1860. Census records suggest he moved to Newcastle as a young boy, probably before the age of ten. He lived with his parents and younger brother on Cut Bank in Byker. His father was a dairyman, and Alec worked at the dairy before starting a new profession as a school teacher. He began playing for Rangers around 1880, at the club's then-home of St James' Park. It's likely that White played in the first ever football match played on the ground, in October 1880. Around the time of his switch to East End, Alec got married, to Jessie, and moved to Heaton, to number 27 Cardigan Terrace, just off Heaton Road. The couple went on to have four children, but Jessie would die in her early 40s leaving Alec as a lone parent.

On the football field, White had been a standout player for Rangers, and had already been selected for the Northumberland FA side. He was a powerful, bustling player, a strong runner with a fierce shot. There was little flair to his game, but that wasn't required at a time when clout beat finesse almost every time. Although a 'scientific' passing game was rapidly gaining popularity in White's native Scotland, the English game was a more basic affair that pretty much revolved around charges and scrimmages. Talented individuals like White, who could win possession, withstand tough challenges, surge past opponents, and shoot strong and true, were much sought-after. It says something about the growing reputation of East End that a player of his standing would have chosen to join them after Rangers folded. As an adopted East Ender, he chose his local team over West End, Tyne Association and others.

White played a major part in pushing East End to the next level. He played for the club for eight seasons, and remained associated with it behind the scenes long after it changed its name to Newcastle United. As the *Newcastle Daily Journal* (now just *The Journal*) would later comment, 'Alec is a general favourite in football circles, and to him is largely owing the prominent position which East End have taken among northern clubs.' And he was a winner. He'd already won silverware with Rangers, and he quickly did the same with East End.

The first trophy won by the club that would become Newcastle United was the Northumberland FA Challenge Cup (now known as the Northumberland Senior Cup), in March 1885. The cup campaign was a tough one. East End beat Elswick Leather Works and Brunswick Villa Athletic to set up a semi-final clash with crosstown rivals West End. The match, a 'rare old game', was played at Heaton Junction – a venue that would come to play a very significant role in the history of the club.

A large crowd of around 1,500 fans saw East End take a 3-1 lead, only for West End to fight back to draw 3-3. Alec White scored twice for East End. The side's other scorer was John Armstrong, who was now one of only two remaining founding players from the Stanley FC days. The other remaining founder was John Cook, a forward who this season was listed as playing at 'centre', making him perhaps the first in an illustrious line of Newcastle centre-forwards.

An East versus West replay, at the Tyne Association ground in Jesmond, saw East End secure a very comfortable 5-0 victory over a disorganised West End, with Alec White again scoring twice – one of his goals a brilliant solo effort that saw him run from his own half, beat the entire West End defence, then smash the ball between the posts.

The cup final was played on 21 March 1885, again at the Tyne Association ground, 'in front of a very large number of spectators'. The opponents were Sleekburn Wanderers, from near Bedlington. 'Opinion was very evenly divided as to the winner of the tie,' reported the *Morpeth Herald*, 'the town club perhaps being the better favourites.'

East End played the first half downhill with the wind and sun at their backs, but failed to score 'owing to bad shooting'. Sleekburn were temporarily reduced to ten men due to an injury, but 'did not lose heart' and 'played up like demons'. In the second half, East End continued to press, and Charles Gorman eventually scored, 'amid tremendous cheering'. A second goal was disallowed for offside, and a 'very fast and exciting game' finally came to an end. East End had won 1-0, and the Northumberland Challenge Cup was presented to John Armstrong. The club he had co-founded had won its first trophy.

More silverware swiftly followed, with East End

winning the Northumberland Charity Shield. The club whupped Sleekburn 6-0 in the semi-final, and then thrashed the Newcastle FA side 10-0 in the final, at the Tyne Association ground. Teddy Hiscock and Tommy Hoban both scored hat-tricks. Gorman scored again, as did White and Armstrong, and William Blackett was the other goalscorer. The gate money from the match went to local charities.

East End had won two trophies in one season – and they could have made it three, only to lose 1-0 to Darlington in the Northumberland and Durham Inter-County Cup. They played well, but were thwarted by Darlington's famous goalkeeper Arthur Wharton, who 'did good fisting-out to keep his fortress intact'. This was a first taste of losing in a cup final for a club that would later make something of a habit of it.

East End's first taste of silverware increased the reputation and standing of the club, and undoubtedly increased its fledgling following. While winning a couple of local FA trophies might not seem particularly thrilling in today's era of Premier Leagues and Champions Leagues, back then it was an impressive feat. There was no league football, and the only national competition was the FA Cup. East End hadn't yet been invited to participate in that, but their time would come. Meanwhile, they had proved themselves to be the best team in Northumberland, covering the huge area from the Scottish Border down to Durham. More newspaper ink was devoted to East End, as other clubs were squeezed out of the football columns, and in some cases squeezed out of existence. Rangers had already folded, and Tyne Association would soon follow. Football fans looking to watch a decent match in Newcastle now had a clear choice – East End or West End.

News of East End's cup successes must have attracted more fans to Dalton Street. Football as a whole was enjoying what the *Penny Illustrated* newspaper called a 'rapid rise in popular favour'. This was partly down to two important factors. Firstly, legislation now declared that all factory and manual work must end by 2pm on a Saturday. Workers had Saturday afternoons free, and looked for something to fill their time. Secondly, Britain was becoming a nation of readers, thanks to an Education Act that required all children to be taught to read and write. This new appetite for reading created a newspaper boom and, then as now, football made popular content. Football columns expanded, and readers devoured tales of their favourite teams and players.

It's hard to overestimate how important newspapers were to early football fans. There was no radio, television or internet, no match commentaries, Sky Sports or Twitter feeds. Newspapers were your only source of information about your football club. Initially, football news and reports were submitted by club secretaries, but during the 1880s, as football exploded in popularity, newspapers began to send reporters to cover matches, and introduced regular football columns. For fans unable to attend matches in person, newspapers provided a means to follow their teams. This was particularly useful for away matches. Telegraph wires and Carrier pigeons were used to distribute scores around the country, and fans would gather outside newspaper offices for updates from faraway towns.

The main local newspapers for football news in the 1880s were the *Tyneside Daily Echo*, the *Newcastle Daily Journal* and the *Newcastle Daily Chronicle*. The *Daily Echo* folded in 1888, so never got to report on East End's transformation into Newcastle United, but both the *Daily Journal* and the *Daily Chronicle* still cover United today, albeit with slightly truncated titles on their mastheads. Slightly further afield, East End's fortunes were covered in the Darlington-based *Northern Echo*, and the *Sunderland Daily Echo*.

The *Chronicle* was owned by Blaydon brickmaker-turned-MP Joseph Cowen, of whom a statue now stands opposite Newcastle's Assembly Rooms on Westgate Road. The popular Cowen was regarded at the time as an unofficial 'King of the Geordies'. The *Chronicle* offices were originally located on Westgate Road, near to where the Cowen statue stands today, and the *Journal* offices were on Clayton Street. After an away match, this is where fans would come to find out the score.

By the mid-1880s, as well as printing team news and match reports, newspapers began to feature early examples of transfer gossip and punditry. Football columns became vibrant message boards for fans, club officials and even players, who wrote in to argue about team selections and complain about refereeing decisions. The newspaper football column often resembled a 19th century version of a modern football phone-in. It was common for columnists to write under football-inspired pen names like 'Goal-Post' or 'Spectator'. Among the first North East football columnists were the *Northern Echo*'s

'Off-Side', and the *Journal*'s 'Custos' (a Latin-derived reference to a goalkeeper).

Custos was quite a character, and one particular passage, from an 1889 column, sums up the colourful and playful style that characterised a lot of early football coverage. Football's many clichés had yet to be coined, and reporters regularly invented new terms with which to describe aspects of the game. 'I have often been amused in reading reports of football matches to see the synonyms which youthful scribes adopt for describing the ball,' wrote Custos. '"The leather", "the globe", the cylinder", "the oval", "the orb of the game", "the greasy roller" and such terms are familiar. But a Sunderland reporter on Saturday took the entire bakery by calling the ball "the coriaceous sphere". If this sort of thing continues, "a scientific exposition of the game" will be something more than a mere phrase. I am told, however, that this is only a sample of what is usually done at Sunderland.'

How many fans, hands and faces still grubby from work, came up to Dalton Street from the shipyards and factories, with a rolled-up copy of the *Journal* in their pockets, to see this exciting team they had read so much about kick around 'the greasy roller'? This was the first generation of Newcastle United fans, a generation that helped to establish the club, supported it, fell in love with it, and handed that support and love down to future generations. The seeds of the club's current support were being sown.

Thinking about it, it's possible that many modern Newcastle United supporters are directly descended from those Victorian East End fans. I've certainly spent time looking back through my family tree, wondering if any of my ancestors were among those early fans who stood around that muddy touch-line in Byker back in the 1880s. Each one of us has two grandfathers, four great-grandfathers, 16 great-great-grandfathers and so on. So by the time you get back to the Victorian era, and combine great-times-whatever-grandfathers with great-grandmothers and great-uncles and great-aunts and various other generations-ago relations, you've got a huge web of ancestors from various places and with various interests. Which among them was it that first fell in love with football, and with the club that would become Newcastle United?

Back on the pitch, as the 1880s reached their midway point, John Armstrong handed the East End captaincy to Alec White – a move that made perfect sense given White's standing in the local game. Although East End were knocked out of the 1885/86 Northumberland FA Challenge Cup by rivals West End (with White playing despite being 'severely indisposed'), they did manage to retain the Northumberland Charity Shield, by beating Morpeth Harriers 2-1.

It was another small triumph for a club that was growing as quickly as the housing and industry surrounding it. The Dalton Street ground was being swallowed up by new terraced streets, and in any case it just wasn't suitable for a club of such growing stature. So, in 1886, East End moved home again, this time to Heaton.

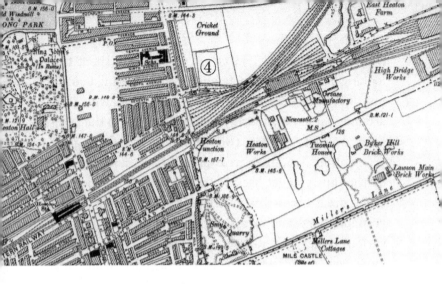

Map of Heaton (c.1898) showing location of Heaton Junction ground (4), north of the railway junction, off Chillingham Road

Location of Heaton Junction ground, off Chillingham Road, at the corner of Spencer and Hartford Streets (photo Paul J White)

*East End FC pictured at their Heaton Junction ground, c.1892
The earliest photo of the team that became Newcastle United
In playing kit, left to right; back row: Bobby Creilly, Peter
Watson, Matt Scott, William Wilson, James Miller, Joe McKane;
front row: John Barker, Tom Crate, Willie Thompson, Jock
Sorley, Joe Wallace. Harry Jeffrey is behind Creilly in a cap*

3

The Heatonians

The half-mile or so journey from Dalton Street to East End's next ground takes us via Shields Road, the main drag between Byker and Heaton. What was once a thriving shopping street now operates in somewhat reduced circumstances. It was originally built as a toll road between Newcastle and North Shields, but by the time football came to town Shields Road was the beating heart of a rapidly-growing community, no doubt bustling with pedestrians and the odd horse-drawn carriage, or 'brake'.

Trade directories for the time show scores of retail establishments on Shields Road, including grocers, drapers, confectioners, butchers, watchmakers, bootmakers and tobacconists. There were also at least three pubs – the Hope and Anchor, the Heaton Hotel and the Raby Hotel. There are still pubs called the Heaton Hotel and the Raby on Shields Road today, although they don't share anything much more than a name with the original incarnations.

North of Shields Road is Heaton, probably best known nationally as the birthplace of TV talent show treasure Cheryl Cole, who was born here in 1983, almost a hundred years after East End moved to the area. Heaton means High Town, and it's situated right up on the bank above the Ouseburn. We're still just a ten minute bus ride from the city centre, and it's also on the Metro line.

With all due respect to Byker, East End were moving up in the world. While Byker was predominantly working class, Victorian Heaton was home to many of Newcastle's upwardly-mobile middle class. Today, Heaton is a pretty vibrant and diverse residential area. Heaton's Chillingham Road, running between Shields Road and the Coast Road, offers a lively mixture of residential homes, grocers, butchers, cafes, and pubs – in many ways not too dissimilar to how it would have been in the 1880s. It's easy to picture this area as it would have been back then, as many of the Victorian terraces that were being built during East End's time in Heaton are still standing, branching away from Chillingham Road as numbered avenues.

East End's new ground – and this time it was most definitely a football *ground* rather than just a football pitch – was at Heaton Junction, on the Newcastle to Edinburgh railway line, just off Chillingham Road, at the corner of Spencer Street and Hartford Street. These streets still survive, and it's easy to imagine fans turning off 'Chilli Road' and thronging into the narrow approach of Hartford Street. The area is now partly covered by terraced housing and a derelict concrete railway yard. Again, there's nothing to suggest that this was once one of the most important locations in the city.

The ground was situated at the former location of the Heaton Athletic Club's bicycle track. Nestled right next to the railway line, the land was owned by the railway company, and in later years was used to house sheds and sidings. Football had been played here previously, but East End turned it into a proper ground, installing fencing, removing the cycle track, and eventually building a timber pavilion, and even a press box. ('Three cheers for East End! Hip-pip-pip!' wrote the *Journal*'s Custos. 'They have erected a shelter in which the reporters may transact their duties screened from the inclemency of the weather.')

Once it was finished, East End's Heaton Junction ground was considered to be far superior than the one used by cross-city rivals West End – a sloping, boggy field just north of the old Newcastle city walls that they'd inherited from the Newcastle Rangers club. (Custos cheekily suggested that West End may eventually emulate East End by erecting a press box 'some time next century'.)

After moving to Heaton in 1886, East End's first match saw them beat West End 3-2 in front of around 2,000 spectators – a massive increase over the crowds attracted to Dalton Street. To extend the comparison with modern day football attendances, we're now getting up to Conference level. The ground was formally opened in October 1886 before a match between East End and Darlington St Augustine's. East End secretary JT Oliver was given the honour of starting the ball, 'before a large assemblage of spectators', and the game finished 2-2. The *Northern Echo* match report concluded: 'The teams after the match dined together at the Heaton Restaurant, where an enjoyable evening was spent.'

Heaton soon became East End's accepted home, and they began to be referred to in press reports as 'the Heatonians' or 'the Heatonites'. The area was rapidly expanding, with hundreds of houses being built on either side of Chillingham Road. As the population of Heaton grew, so did East End's attendances. Football was still an emerging game, and anywhere outside of a big FA Cup tie an attendance of 2,000 or more was pretty good going.

Naturally, matches between East End and West End drew Newcastle's biggest crowds, as the rivalry between the two clubs developed. This eclipsed any early Tyne-Wear football rivalry with Sunderland. The Wearside club had their own rivals in breakaway club Sunderland Albion. At the heart of these early rivalries was the growing realisation that each city could only really support one top club. In 1887 Tyne Association, Newcastle's oldest club, folded. These early clubs were battling not just for local supremacy, but for survival.

There was still little to separate East End and West End, and there was regular parity on the pitch. One snowy day in March 1887, West End crossed the city to East End's Heaton Junction ground, only to find a notice posted on the gates announcing that the match would not take place due to the pitch being covered with snow. East End had apparently sent a message to West End, but the news had been 'miscarried'. Luckily, a few East End players, including Alec White, were at the ground. They managed to pull together an eleven, and the game was played in the snow. It ended as a 1-1 draw.

In October 1887 East End took the big step into national competition, as for the first time they entered the

FA Cup. They faced tough opposition in the first qualifying round in the shape of long-established Teesside club South Bank, which had been formed way back in 1868. East End travelled to Paradise Field in Middlesbrough for the game on 17 October. The ground had been soaked by heavy rain, and 'many nasty spills were witnessed'. East End fell behind, then equalised twice, with William Muir scoring both goals for the Heatonians. At full-time the score was 2-2 and the referee (a Mr J Bastard, if you can believe that) ordered that an extra half-hour should be played.

Extra-time was very even, with 'each team putting forth their best efforts'. The game was finally settled in the 112th minute, when a South Bank forward named Jones dribbled up the right wing, cut between the East End backs, and scored 'a cleverly got goal'. 3-2 to South Bank, and East End were out of the FA Cup after their first tie.

East End fared better in the Northumberland Challenge Cup, and in a first round match in January 1888 registered the club's biggest ever victory – an enduring Newcastle United record that stands to this day. The opponents were Point Pleasant, a small club from Wallsend, and the venue was a packed Heaton Junction. Despite the fact that East End fielded a 'very weak' team due to the absence of several regular players, they pinned the visitors in their own half 'from start to finish'.

Somehow, an 'aggressive' East End failed to score for the first 15 minutes, with the Point Pleasant players packing their goalmouth. Then some neat passing allowed White to break the deadlock. Scott immediately scored a second goal, and then Hiscock added a third, apparently without any Pleasant player touching the ball other than to kick off. By half-time the score was 6-0 to East End. And in the second half, incredibly, the Heatonians added another 13 goals. Newspapers spelled out the remarkable scoreline: 'East End: Nineteen Goals, Point Pleasant: None.'

'But for the splendid display of the visitors' custodian the score would have been much larger,' reported the *Morpeth Herald*. Alec White scored nine of his side's goals. Andy Muir scored four, Scott and Hiscock both scored two, and Wakefield scored the other goal. The 19-0 win eclipses Newcastle United's 'official' biggest win, 13-0 against Newport County in 1946. And Alec White's nine goals against Point Pleasant betters Len Shackleton's six against County. Once again, the club's pre-1892 history reveals achievements that deserve to be better remembered.

That big win, though, was the high point in a pretty disappointing season. Indicating the uneven and unpredictable nature of early North East football, East End were knocked out of the Northumberland Challenge Cup in the next round by Elswick Rangers, losing 3-1 at Heaton. It looked like East End were on the slide, and with local rivals jostling for supremacy and survival, that slide had to be halted.

The turnaround began when East End acquired hugely influential secretary Tom Watson from West End. Watson had been forced out of the West End club after an FA Cup tie at St James' Park between local side Shankhouse and Aston Villa. Villa won 9-0, but overcrowding in the ground let to pitch incursions and a delayed kick-off. As the secretary in charge of the venue, Watson was deemed responsible, and he subsequently left West End. His move across the city was a huge boost to East End.

In the Victorian era, the club secretary generally arranged fixtures, kept records and submitted match details to local papers. But Watson went way beyond that remit, getting involved in player recruitment, team selection and tactics. He was a football manager in all but name, before such a post really existed.

He pioneered the recruitment of players from Scotland, crossing the border at great personal risk at a time when player-poachers from English clubs were known to be trussed up and ducked in barrels of water. Tempting players with the offer of a decent job in Newcastle and a £5 signing-on fee, Watson quickly improved East End. He would later become regarded as the first great football manager, helping to establish two other big English clubs. But his first impressive act was to establish East End as the best club in the North East.

In 1888/89 East End achieved a remarkable local treble of the Northumberland Challenge Cup, Northumberland Charity Shield and Northumberland and Durham Inter County Cup. The Challenge Cup was won in curious circumstances. The final, against Elswick Rangers, ended in a goalless draw. 'The game produced very little skill, as the teams showed more spleen than anything else,' reported the *Northern Echo*. East End lost the replay 2-1, but Elswick had fielded an ineligible player, and the match was ordered to be played again.

The second replay took place at the neutral venue of

St James' Park on 13 April in front of around 5,000 spectators. East End took a 3-0 lead through goals from Teddy Hiscock, James Collins and a centre-forward called Mack, whose first name seems to have been lost to history. Elswick fought back to 3-2, but East End held on for victory. 'Alec White was as full of dash as ever, and played a rattling game,' reported the *Journal*.

After the match, Elswick attempted to turn the tables by complaining that East End had this time fielded an ineligible player, but the protest was rejected. The aggrieved Elswick then refused to face East End in the Charity Shield final, so that trophy was awarded to the Heatonians by default.

Controversy continued into the Northumberland and Durham Cup final, against Sunderland Albion. The match was played at Blue House Field, the original ground of Sunderland AFC, of which Sunderland Albion was a breakaway club. East End won a tight match 1-0, thanks to a deflection off an Albion defender, confirming the club's unlikely 'treble'.

Albion weren't happy, though, that the joint-association match should be decided by an own goal. They demanded a swift rematch. Despite the fact that the football season had ended, the rematch was arranged for the following week, this time at Heaton Junction. Again, East End won 1-0.

It was Alec White's last match for the club. He was only 29, but the tough Victorian game had no doubt made his limbs feel much older. And he'd ended his East End career as he'd started it – by winning silverware. At a special celebration dinner in Heaton, East End's players were presented with their cups and medals after an unprecedented treble-winning season. White was presented with a pocket watch to mark his retirement. He'd still be around, watching from the sidelines, as the club continued its progress.

It's worth remembering that East End was still an amateur club at this point. The players all had 'proper' jobs, and weren't officially paid for playing football. In fact, until the mid-1880s it was actually illegal to pay footballers. The decision to legalise professionalism – a decision effectively forced upon the FA by ambitious clubs in the summer of 1885 – would change football forever, marking an inevitable shift towards commercialism. But although East End had found success on the field, and had a growing following, a calendar of friendly matches and the occasional cup tie wasn't really enough to sustain a commercial business.

It was this very problem that prompted Aston Villa director William McGregor to initiate the formation of the Football League in 1888. The league provided its 12 original members with a reliable income stream that allowed them to pay their players, improve their grounds, increase their attendances, and ultimately thrive. A testament to the success of the Football League is the fact that, of the 12 founding members, 11 still exist today. (The exception is Accrington FC, not to be confused with Accrington Stanley.)

East End didn't have a high enough profile to be invited to join the Football League – in fact no North East clubs were invited to join. But East End's Tom Watson recognised that league football was the way forward for his club. He proposed a meeting to form a North East-based league. However, in the week that Watson's proposal was printed in newspapers, it was announced that football officials in Darlington had beaten him to the punch, and formed what is now the second-oldest football league in the world – the Northern League.

East End joined the Northern League as a founder member in 1889. They also became a professional outfit, and began to officially pay their players, although the players would have retained their original jobs. We know that at this time the East End team were training on evenings once or twice a week, and they could carry on working in the factories, down the mines, or on the river, heading straight from work on a Saturday lunchtime to play for East End on a Saturday afternoon.

The East End that entered the Northern League was an organised and forward-thinking club, and the future must have seemed bright. But, before the opening Northern League season could get underway, East End were dealt a major blow when they lost Tom Watson to Sunderland.

Watson, highly-regarded, according the *Sunderland Daily Echo*, for his 'unrivalled knowledge of footballers and their ways', was approached in a Newcastle pub and offered £100 a year and a new suit to swap Tyneside for Wearside. He accepted, and soon got Sunderland elected to the national Football League. The club's deep pockets allowed him to recruit the very best Scottish players, and build the 'Team of all Talents' that would win the league three times. Watson remains to this day Sunderland's most successful manager. He subsequently won the league twice with Liverpool, meaning he played a major part in building three of English football's biggest clubs. Yet he remains another Newcastle football pioneer whose name is barely remembered today.

Their first Northern League match, on 7 September 1889, saw the East End players entertain 1,500 spectators with a 45-minute display of ball skills while they waited for the delayed Darlington team to arrive. Although the Heaton ground was located at a railway junction, passenger trains stopped at Newcastle's Central Station, and visiting teams travelled from there in horse-drawn brakes or charabancs. When they finally arrived, the Darlington players were greeted with a huge roar, and then beaten 2-1 courtesy of two goals from James Miller.

East End had three players called J Miller in 1889 – one James and two Johns. The *Northern Echo* cheerfully reported this fact in its 'Dressing Room Chat' football gossip column, alongside transfer rumours, questions about financial transactions, and the fact that 'six members of the Sunderland team, including [John] Auld, are teetotallers, and there are seven non-smokers'.

James Miller seems to have started out as a forward, before moving to left-back. The two John Millers played inside-left and outside-right. All three J Millers scored in a 3-1 win over Middlesbrough in September 1889. Newspapers reported the East End scorers as 'J Miller (1)', 'J Miller (2)' and 'J Miller (3)'.

James Miller was a key player for East End, and would play for the club right through until 1893, after it changed its name to Newcastle United. One of Tom Watson's Scottish imports, signed from Kilmarnock, Miller took over the East End captaincy from Alec White, who had retired from playing in 1889. Miller's less-than-unusual name makes obtaining personal information about him tricky, but from census records it looks like he was born in Scotland in 1869, and was 20 when East End joined the Northern League. Photographic evidence shows that he was one of the few East End players who didn't wear a moustache.

We do know that James Miller was something of a hothead. He was suspended by the FA for six weeks following the Middlesbrough match for unspecified 'misconduct on the field'. He was also the first East End player to be recorded as being sent off, after a bust-up with West End's John Barker in a Newcastle derby.

Barker would soon join Miller at East End, and had already played for the Heatonians back in December 1887. East End had been unable to raise a full team to face Darlington at Feethams, and borrowed four players from West End. The West Enders – Taylor, Swinburne, McDonald and Barker – were named by the *Northern Echo* as Newcastle's best performers, but the combined might of East and West still lost 5-2. Newcastle's goalscorers were East Enders Hoban and Scott. Nevertheless, this 'united' Newcastle team was a curious precursor of what was to come.

Although election to the Northern League helped East End to improve, they still had a long way to go. Now shorn of Alec White, and without the recruitment skills of Tom Watson, the team lacked real quality. As the *Morpeth Herald* commented, 'They are scarcely as good as they were a few years ago, but their best days may be yet to come.'

Tom Watson returned to Heaton Junction in November 1889 with his Sunderland team. 'The East End ground, if smaller than at Sunderland, is level and well adapted to play,' reported the *Sunderland Echo*. 'The game was timed to begin at 2.45pm. The weather was brilliant, and there were some 2,000 spectators. The Sunderland team arrived 20 minutes late, owing, it was rumoured, to having been driven to the wrong field.'

It was a terrible day for fans of the Heatonians, as Sunderland raced to a 3-0 half-time lead. 'Cries of "Play up East End" were of little avail, for the better team were showing the way,' said the *Echo*. The final score was 4-0 to the Wearsiders, and it was clear that Watson was having a positive impact at his new club. But if East End were still unable to compete with Sunderland, they could at least push for dominance on Tyneside.

By now the club had built up a regular following of spectators, paying 6d (£1.50 in today's money) to gain admission, and were in a position where they could issue season tickets. They also had travelling fans who would take 'football special' trains or 'brake club' charabancs to away matches in their hundreds. There was also a rowdy element among the East End support. A December 1890 defeat against Middlesbrough, watched by 'a good attendance of spectators', was blighted by crowd trouble. After receiving a report from the referee, the Northumberland Association ordered East End to place posters around the Heaton Junction ground warning spectators about their future conduct, otherwise matches at the ground would be suspended.

For one home match in 1889, the club reduced its admission fee in an attempt to increase attendance. It didn't work. 'In the East End and Middlesbrough match, the former club tried a threepenny gate by way of experiment,' reported the *Northern Echo*, 'with the result that it was considerably less than half the amount taken at the sixpenny admission when the Darlington team played.'

Around this time, East End were fielding players who could be considered to be genuine stars – at least by the club's growing band of supporters. Between the posts, Matt Scott was regarded as one of the best goalkeepers in the Northern League. Up front, Willie Thompson was a nippy little centre-forward from the town that would later produce Jackie Milburn, and Jack and Bobby Charlton - Ashington. Thompson scored around 65 goals for the club, which might quite not put him in Milburn's league but is still pretty impressive. Along with half-backs Bobby Creilly and Joe McKane, forwards Jock Sorley and Joe Wallace, and the afore-mentioned James Miller, Thomson would continue to star for the club after it became known as Newcastle United.

In 1890, East End took the major step of becoming a limited company, issuing 1,600 shares at 10 shillings each (worth the equivalent of £48,000 in total or £30 each today). Prospective shareholders could pay in two instalments – five shillings on application and another five on allocation. The idea was, as the *Chronicle* reported, to 'make the scheme more popular and within reach of the working classes'. The shares were sold in local pubs in Heaton and Byker, as the club effectively became fan-owned.

All of those fans were local, and many of them were working class. Examination of East End's share returns shows that every single East End shareholder lived within three miles of the club's Heaton base. Shareholders' professions were also listed on the returns. A breakdown of the returns published in the *Soccer and Society* journal classifies 40% of East End's shareholders as manual workers, 25% as clerks, managers or foremen, 29% as employers or proprietors, and 4% as professionals. (These figures only add up to 98% due to the journal's rounding.)

The returns show that only one East End shareholder was a woman – Mary Laing bought two shares for a total of 20 shillings. Former players, including Alec White, John Armstrong and John Dixon, also bought shares. All three were among the club's first directors. Armstrong and Dixon had been founder members of Stanley FC, indicating that at least a few of those once-young lads were still involved as the club continued to grow. Now East End wasn't just representing the local community – it was owned by it.

Across town, at their St James' Park ground, West End also became a limited company, but the club began to struggle on and off the pitch. Having previously been shoulder-to-shoulder rivals, East End began to shove West End aside. In September 1890 East End thrashed West End 7-1 at Heaton Junction. The Heatonians were now Newcastle's dominant club, and it was the beginning of the end for their rivals.

East End continued to forge ahead. They had a decent team, a growing band of supporters, and financial stability. They improved the Heaton Junction ground, and switched shirt colours – from blue to red. A wonderful photo exists showing the East End team, lined up in their red shirts and white knickers, in front of the Heaton Junction pavilion, which is packed with moustachioed gents in felt bowler hats – plus a handful of ladies in their fineries. These are the posh seats, and the folk in them represent the more well-to-do Heatonians, but the photo gives us a fascinating first glimpse of early Newcastle United fans.

The average league match attendance at the Heaton Junction ground was more than 3,000, and that number could be swelled to as many as 6,000 or even 8,000 for FA Cup ties. A real bond had developed between local people and the club. 'The cheering of the crowd at any good play on the part of the East End men showed the pride the Heatonians take in their team,' said the *Journal* after a match between East End and West End. The team was representing its community against rivals from across town and further afield, and was giving a pretty good account of itself. No wonder spectators showed their pride, and turned up in increasing numbers.

Looking back as modern day football fans, it's quite possible to understand why attendances increased so quickly, and how our ancestors became hooked on the game. As a *Daily News* reporter wrote in 1892, 'Nobody who witnesses a match between first class teams can wonder at the hold which football has obtained upon the affections of the people, and few would go away without having suddenly acquired an interest in the game.'

The fact that East End – like many English clubs – were increasingly recruiting players from Scotland meant that the team was no longer made up of local lads. But in an era long before footballers became highly-paid superstars, the new recruits lived right among their supporters, so fans were still cheering on their neighbours.

'Nowadays, it is true, most of the Northern Association teams are composed of invaders from across the Border,' wrote the sportsman and writer CB Fry, 'but these are soon identified with their new home, and become to all intents and purposes natives.'

By 1892 East End had established themselves as the top club in Newcastle, and one of the top three or four clubs in the North East. They were still some way behind the dominant Middlesbrough Ironopolis, and literally leagues behind Football League side Sunderland. However, an opportunity was about to arise that would change things forever.

Looking back at these earliest days of Newcastle United, what's most notable is how very ordinary the club's beginnings were. This was a football club set up by a bunch of working class kids – a group of mates who played cricket together and developed an enthusiasm for the new Association game. The fact that Stanley/East End survived and thrived while so many other local clubs had very short lives could be down to the enthusiasm and tenacity of those involved, or it could be down to luck. It was probably a little bit of both, combined with an appetite from the people of Byker, Heaton and the surrounding areas for an exciting new sport.

Our time in Heaton is coming to an end, so we can turn back along Hartford Street towards Chillingham

Road, imagining the voices of 6,000 spectators cheering on their team behind us. *'Play up, East End!'* A young lad rides past on a delivery bike with an insulated pizza bag on the handlebars. There's a bloke carefully studying a betting coupon as he walks, and then, unusually, a pair of uniformed flight attendants trundling cabin bags towards the Metro. It's tempting to yell at them, 'Hey! This is where Newcastle United used to play!' But they have pizzas to deliver and bets to place and flights to catch. And they'd probably think you were nuts. So it's best to just button the lip and shift on.

You'll notice that we're 60-odd pages in to this story now and we're only just reaching 1892. We've gone from Stanley FC to East End, and from Byker to Heaton, via four grounds. There have been lots of good players and a handful of great ones. The club has won trophies – actual shiny silver pots of the kind that we modern supporters might never have laid eyes on in service to our football club. Most importantly, it's built up a fanbase and begun to *matter* to people. Already, this delve into history has provided evidence for the beginnings of the enduring connection between the fans and the club, and we haven't even got to the bit where it becomes Newcastle United yet. To get there we need to follow East End to Newcastle city centre, to a famous football ground, and to something of a union between East and West.

In the 1891/92 season East End beat West End home and away. In May 1892, after struggling with finances for more than a year, West End was disbanded, and the lease on their ground was up for grabs. East End were under pressure from the railway company over rent increases and the possible redevelopment of Heaton Junction. The decision was made: East End would move away from Heaton into the city centre, and take over West End's vacated lease. East End moved to St James' Park.

Tom Watson
East End secretary/manager

Map (c.1899) showing the location of St James' Park, between Gallowgate and Leazes Park, and adjacent to St James' Street

St James' Park from Barrack Road, and Leazes Terrace

'Woolwich Arsnel [sic] v Newcastle United', the Football League debut for both sides, at the Manor Ground in Plumstead, 1893

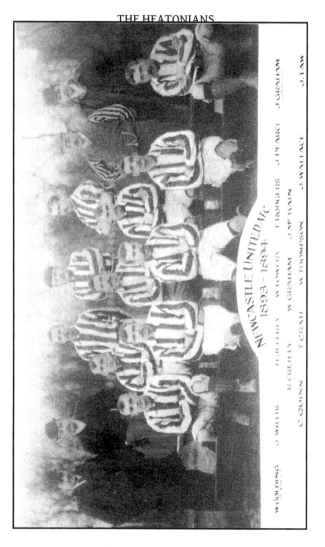

Newcastle United team postcard, 1893-1894
Newcastle's first season in the Football League, and in black
and white stripes. Pictured in playing kit left to right; back row:
Harry Jeffrey, W Lowery, Tom Rodger(s); middle row: Bobby
Creilly, Willie Graham, Joe McKane; front row: C Quinn, Tom
Crate, Willie Thompson, Joe Wallace, John Law

4

St James' Park

I'm biased of course, but this place is more than a bit special. Packed with believers and full of noise, illuminated by floodlights and throbbing with passion, it's a thrilling place to be on a matchday. Even empty, early on a weekday morning, St James' Park retains an impressive feel and standing that make it deserving of its place in the hearts of football fans, and at the heart of this great city.

St James' occupies a lofty position at the north west of Newcastle city centre, just outside the old town walls. You can see it from pretty much everywhere in and around the city (being as it is 210 feet high), serving as a constant reminder of the fact that football courses through the city as sure as does the Tyne.

When you've been coming here since you were a kid, when you've been here many hundreds of times, so many time that you feel completely at home here, it's easy to take it for granted. But from my vantage point at the old town walls, just a goal-kick from the hill on which St James' stands, a quick crane of the neck upwards serves as a suitable reminder of what a magnificent place it is. If this was a posh book, this might be an opportune time to mention Proustian rushes and all that, but it isn't, so let's just say that gazing up at St James' Park gives me a proper thrill. The hairs on the back of my neck are standing on end. (I really must ask a barber to do something about those hairs.)

The ground has changed almost completely even since I started coming here in the mid-1980s. Back then, both the Gallowgate and Leazes ends were open standing terraces, and the Edwardian West Stand was still in place. Only the East Stand, built in 1973, remains today. Now the Milburn Stand to the west and the Sir John Hall Stand to the north are 15 storeys high, and covered by a sweeping glass roof. The south stand is the Gallowgate, where I stood on the terrace as a kid, and that's the nearest stand to this vantage point at the walls.

Newcastle's town walls were built in the 13th century to repel those pesky marauding Scots. Originally more than 20 feet high and eight feet thick in places, they did their job for 400 years or so, but were finally breached during the brutal siege of the town in 1644. Newcastle was loyal to King Charles during the English Civil War, and was besieged by Scottish troops allied with Oliver Cromwell's Parliamentarians. The invading army was 30,000 strong, while Newcastle had only 1,700 defenders – 800 trained soldiers from the garrison plus 900 volunteer townsfolk.

One Scottish eyewitness called the town's inhabitants 'a *masse* of silly ignorants', which wasn't very nice (although to be fair we've been called a lot worse since). Despite a fierce onslaught of skirmish raids, cannon fire and grenades – coupled with a severe lack of food, water and other supplies – Newcastle managed to hold out for three months, with the Parliamentarians cursing the town's '*obstinacie*'.

The nearby St Andrew's Church took a pounding during the siege, but still stands today. There are three cannonballs inside the church as proof of its ordeal. Records show that cannon fire breached the town walls near to St Andrew's, although the townsfolk were quick to repair the damage with timber. From this viewpoint, it seems likely that the Scots would have placed their cannons up on the hill pretty much exactly where St James' Park now stands, overlooking the town that so belligerently defied them.

For its heroics during the civil war, King Charles bestowed Newcastle with its motto: *Fortiter Defendit Triumphans* (Triumph by Brave Defence). I've often though that certain Newcastle United managers should probably have been more aware of that motto.

By the time St James' Park was created in the 1880s the walls had mostly been demolished, but the longest remaining section is right here, running parallel to Stowell Street, which is now the heart of the city's Chinatown. Unfortunately, the walls have become a bit of a rubbish dump, and a place for some genuine 'silly ignorants' to chuck away their empty super-strength lager tins.

A bus trundles past the nearby Chinatown gates, and a couple of students wander into a fried chicken shop. A beer barrel clangs against tarmac as a driver unloads his truck outside the Tyneside Irish Centre. I head across Gallowgate and up towards St James' Park, which may hitherto occasionally be referred to as SJP.

The Gallowgate road runs along the north-west corner of the town walls, and is so named because condemned prisoners would be led along here from the gaol at Newgate to 'the fatal tree' at Gallows Hole – located, as far as records suggest, at the exact site of SJP. Thieves, murderers and suspected witches were all hung at Gallows Hole, often in front of large crowds. So SJP has long been a venue for spectator sports.

The last hanging here was in 1844 (although hangings continued elsewhere in Newcastle until 1919), when a crowd gathered in front of Leazes Terrace to watch Mark Sherwood hang for the brutal murder of his wife Ann. (He had cut off her head in their house on Blandford Street.)

The name of Gallowgate is so strongly associated with SJP that it's sometimes used as shorthand for the ground itself. The Gallowgate is to SJP what the Kop is to Anfield, although various ground developments and seat moves mean the Gallowgate end is no longer necessarily the traditional home of the club's most fervent fans.

Walking across Gallowgate and up to the ground, past the Sir Bobby Robson memorial garden, and the St James Metro station (*without* an apostrophe, punctuation fans), you reach The Strawberry pub and Strawberry Place, named, fairly obviously, because this was once the site of strawberry fields. (As far as I can tell, however, Newcastle has never had a Penny Lane.)

There's been a pub on this street corner almost as long as the ground has been here, and The Strawberry is a traditional pre-match haunt – if you can get in. On match days it's usually rammed – you could easily pop a rib or two squeezing past densely packed punters on the way to the bar. On non-match days like this, The Strawberry reveals itself as a very decent traditional pub of the like that are rapidly disappearing in the city. It's filled to the rafters with NUFC photos, shirts and other memorabilia, the pub sign that hangs outside is a black and white shirt with a big strawberry on it, and SJP is just a cheeky back-heel away.

The Strawberry is no longer the nearest pub to SJP, although it remains the most authentic. After the redevelopment of the Leazes end, a new bar was installed in the back of the stand – originally given the name Shearer's, but now known as Nine. Next to Nine is the NUFC Official Store. Next to the store, outside SJP's 'Strawberry corner', stands another recent addition, or more accurately recent re-location, namely a statue of one of Newcastle's greatest ever players – the legendary Jackie Milburn, who played 395 times for the club between 1943 and 1957, scoring 200 goals. Only Alan Shearer, with 206 goals, has scored more for Newcastle (although, if you include his 38 wartime goals, Milburn comes out on top). 'Wor Jackie' won the FA Cup three times with Newcastle, in 1951, 1952 and 1955. Looking back on that achievement from a modern era of lean pickings makes it seem all the more remarkable.

The stadium's grey steel framework looms overhead, and the sun is threatening to shine. An ambulance races past with sirens whirring, on the way, no doubt, to the nearby Royal Victoria Infirmary. The RVI was opened in 1906, and so didn't exist when St James' Park was first established. The whole area north of here was once part of the Town Moor. Known as Castle Leazes, the land was presented as a gift to the people of Newcastle in the early 13th century by King John, to be used for cultivation and grazing. Legend has it that freemen of the city, including Alan Shearer, are still entitled to graze their cattle in the area, if they have the inclination.

Newcastle United weren't the first team to play here. Castle Leazes was used for various sports during in the Victorian era, including bowling, quoits, and 'knurr and spell' – a popular bat and ball game. The St James' Park area was turned into a football field in 1880 by Newcastle's Rangers FC – the former club of Alec White. The first match at St James' was played in October 1880 between the Rangers captain's first team and a team of 15 'others'. 'After a pleasant game of two hours it was found that the captain's team was victorious over his numerous but less experienced opponents to the extent of six goals to one,' reported the *Journal*.

Rangers left St James' in 1882, and the field was left mostly unused, only occasionally played on by amateur clubs such as Newcastle Wednesday – who, unsurprisingly, played there every Wednesday. After that, the history of SJP was shaped by a club we've already encountered, Newcastle West End.

While East End were establishing themselves over in Byker and Heaton, West End were doing likewise across town. Like their rivals, West End were formed by cricketers. Crown Cricket Club was established in the Crown Street area of Elswick. Like East End's Stanley Street, Crown Street no longer exists, but it would have been near to Elswick Park, about a mile south-west of SJP. The football team was formed in August 1882, almost a year after Stanley/East End had emerged. It was decided to call the football team West End, and set up home on the Town Moor.

West End played on a pitch at Castle Leazes, but not yet at St James' Park. The site of West End's ground is described as being further north, probably on the area known as Nun's Moor. West End swiftly became a decent amateur team, at least as good as East End. In 1885 the club moved to a new pitch north of Brandling Park in Jesmond. The site, just off the Great North Road, is still used for football today.

Then in 1886 West End moved to St James' Park, erecting an eight-foot wooden fence around the pitch, and turning it into a proper football ground. Press reports from the time called SJP 'very large' and said West End's improvements would make it 'one of the best, if not the best, grounds in the north'. The first match at the 'new' St James' saw West End host East End in front of 2,000 spectators. West End won 3-2 to suitably christen their new home.

Walking up past the south east corner of the ground, we come to the back lane of St James' Street, the very same back lane that those couple of thousand spectators would have walked up and down back in 1886. The lane now has a Tarmac surface, but until very recently it was paved with cobbles, polished to a shiny and slippery finish by more than a hundred years' worth of Newcastle supporters' feet. There were no stands in those early days, although there was a soil embankment along this east side of the ground that was covered in bark chippings for standing on. Later, West End improved SJP by adding the luxury of wooden duckboards to save spectators' boots from getting muddy.

This location gave the ground its name. St James' Park is named simply because of its position next to St James' Street, and the adjoining St James' Terrace. It had been named when Rangers first used the ground, and West End had no reason to change it. There have been several chapels of St James in Newcastle over the years, and the streets were probably named in relation to one of them. Today the street signs show St James Street and St James Terrace – without apostrophes – but Victorian trade directories show they did have apostrophes in the 1880s, hence the St James' Park apostrophe.

That apostrophe has long been a bane to newspaper copy-editors, although the archives show it's been in place since Rangers played at the ground in the early 1880s. The earliest reference in the *Journal* archives is given as 'St James' Park', although the paper did sometimes add a second S to make it 'St James's Park'.

Technically, because it is pronounced 'Saint Jameses Park' rather than 'Saint James Park', it probably should have that second S. The *Guardian* newspaper's modern style guide says, 'The possessive in words and names ending in S normally takes an apostrophe followed by a second S (Jones's, James's), but be guided by pronunciation.' But the great thing about the English language is that it can be bent and shaped in many different ways, particularly by us Geordies.

St James, by the way, was one of the 12 apostles of

Jesus. There were two apostles, some say disciples, named James. 'Ours', the son of Zebedee, was known as 'James the Greater' (as opposed to the son of Alphaeus, who was, unfortunately for him, known as 'James the Less'). Our St James was apparently known for his fiery temper, and he and his brother and fellow disciple John were known as the Sons of Thunder, which sounds a bit like a motorcycle gang, but almost certainly wasn't. James was the first apostle to become a martyr, being beheaded with a sword by King Herod Agrippa around 44 AD. St James, or Santiago, is the patron saint of Spain, and also of veterinarians, tanners and pharmacists.

There are four football grounds named St James' Park in England, but who do they belong to? Most football fans can probably name Newcastle United and Exeter City, therefore winning two out of four points in a pub quiz. Plenty of North East-based fans will pick up a third point by naming Alnwick Town. Alnwick, located just 35 miles north of Newcastle, also play in black and white, and are also nicknamed the Magpies. (Could a connection with Stanley FC co-founder William Coulson, who moved to the Alnwick area, has anything to do with that?)

The fourth club that plays at a St James' Park is, clever clogs and the internet will tell you, Brackley Town of the Football Conference North division. But Newcastle's St James' Park is the original, being established some 20 years before Alnwick's ground, 25 years before Exeter's, and a full 94 years before Brackley's. (Of course, we're only talking about football grounds here – London's public park of the same name (but different spelling – it's St *James's* Park) was established a good 300 years before Newcastle's SJP.)

In 1892 St James' Park became home to Newcastle United, then still called East End. Something we should probably clear up right now is the 'myth of the merger'. There was no merger between East End and West End. It's easy to see how this myth could have arisen, although contemporary sources and several more recent texts do make the truth clear. West End had suffered 'a heavy financial loss', and the club was disbanded. West End directors William Neasham and John Black, 'in sportsmanlike manner', informed the East End board of the situation, and invited them to pick at the bones of the club.

There was, it's true to say, some confusion among supporters at the time. One correspondent wrote to the *Chronicle* enquiring whether or not there had been a merger between East End and West End. On the following day, the newspaper published a response confirming that there had not been a merger, and that the West End club was 'defunct'.

'There was no formal amalgamation,' confirms Arthur Appleton in *Hotbed of Soccer*. 'West End were defunct, although some of their directors joined the East End board, and three of their discarded players were signed on by East End.' Of course, the real jewel left behind by West End was St James' Park. Although Heaton Junction was considered a better ground, St James' had a better location. 'The ground's situation – not far from Central Station and near the centre of the city – was the great attraction,' says Appleton. So it was agreed that East End would leave Heaton and take over the lease at SJP.

Under the headline, 'Goodbye to West End', the *Journal* reported: 'We are informed that the Newcastle West End Club has now ceased to exist... and the executive of the East End club will become the occupiers of St James' Park. With the change of grounds, and increased strength of their elevens for the next season, East End should attract big gates in the future and the financial pressure which has formerly been known should become a thing of the past.'

East End's first match at SJP as the home team was a friendly against Celtic, played on 3 September 1892 in front of 7,000 spectators. Celtic were a big draw, with an exciting team that was about to win the Scottish League for the first time. The match was billed as 'the greatest event known in the local history of the game'. It was decided by a single controversial goal, scored when East End keeper David Whitton, making his debut after joining from the wreckage of West End, was bundled over the goal-line with the ball by Celtic forward Johnny Madden. Although football at the time was pretty rough and tumble, the referee later admitted that the goal shouldn't have stood, but that wasn't much consolation – East End had lost 1-0.

After the money-spinning Celtic match, the East End board must have been mightily disappointed to see attendances at their new ground fall away. Rather than attracting new fans, it seemed that the move to this central location had driven away old ones. 6,000 fans had gone along to see East End play Middlesbrough Ironopolis at Heaton Junction in April 1892, but only 2,000 turned up to see them play Darlington at SJP that November.

This drop in attendance was financially disastrous, but it shouldn't have been surprising.

East End's band of supporters – around 3,000 regulars, including hundreds of season ticket holders, plus another few thousand who attended occasional matches – was primarily based in Byker and Heaton. The move to SJP meant the best part of an hour's walk (or an expensive brake ride) to watch a match. They couldn't really be blamed for staying at home. As for fans of the now-defunct West End, they could also be forgiven for not rushing along to their former home to watch their biggest rivals. Imagine, to provide an admittedly unlikely modern equivalent, if Manchester United folded, and Manchester City moved to Old Trafford. It's fair to assume that fans of both clubs would be pretty miffed.

East End had some bridges to build if they were to unite the supporters of East End and West End behind Newcastle's only remaining professional club. At a meeting on 9 December 1892, it was agreed that the club should change its name. A report in the *Journal* said 'there was a certain amount of jealousy existing among some people regarding the present title of the club, and it was considered that a more general and representative name should be chosen'. The club's directors wanted 'a first class team, and to see the game played as it ought to be, and they all knew that to secure a team to do honour to the city they must have the unanimous support of the public'.

At the important meeting, city councillor Arthur Henderson stood and said that 'the supporters of East End and the old West End would have to sink any little jealousies they had, and be united'. Those gathered responded with a 'Hear, hear'. 'With the support of the whole of the Newcastle sporting public,' the councillor continued, 'they ought to have a team second to none in the country'.

Three names were proposed: Newcastle; Newcastle City; and Newcastle United. A vote was taken, and one name was chosen 'by a large majority'. A motion was carried to change the name, 'with only three dissentients'. East End became Newcastle United.

Newcastle are football's second-oldest United. The first was Sheffield United, formed in 1889. After Newcastle became United in 1892, Thames Ironworks became West Ham United in 1900, and Newton Heath became Manchester United in 1902. So Newcastle were United a full ten years before Manchester adopted the name (which makes it particularly galling when journalists and commentators refer to Newcastle United versus Manchester United matches as 'Newcastle versus United').

Walking up past St James' Street and behind the East Stand, a brutalist grey concrete structure, we reach Leazes Terrace. The Grade I listed development was built in the 1830s by Richard Grainger, who was responsible for creating many of Newcastle's most handsome features. Originally, SJP slotted nicely into the space between Leazes Terrace on the east and Barrack Road on the west, but in later years the 600ft-long Leazes quadrangle has prevented further expansion on this side of the ground.

The grand four-storey terrace was once home to some of Newcastle's most genteel residents, but the Pot

Noodles and posters visible through the windows are clues to the fact that the building is now being used as student digs. The stonework could do with a clean, but it's still a very impressive building, albeit currently existing in somewhat scruffy circumstances. Having the ugly East Stand looming just feet away doesn't help. But most Newcastle supporters would probably admit that knocking down Leazes Terrace, as previous SJP extension plans have proposed, would have been very unfortunate.

There isn't another soul around at the moment, in contrast to match days, when thousands of fans fill the narrow space between the East Stand and Leazes Terrace, turning it into a coursing river of black and white (inevitably with a car stuck hopelessly in the middle of things because the driver apparently didn't realise there was a match on).

The grazing area above Leazes Terrace was developed into parkland during the latter half of the 19th century. Leazes Park is perhaps an underappreciated part of Newcastle upon Tyne. It's a classic Victorian park, opened in 1873 following a petition from working men for 'ready access to some open ground for the purposes of health and recreation'. The park was developed through into the 1890s, at the same time that St James' Park and Newcastle United were being developed next door. The main feature of the park is a boating lake, populated by scores of swans and ducks. Today, fishermen sit patiently in their waterproofs around the lake, and a mother hands a toddler breadcrumbs to throw to the ducks.

St James' Park towers over the southern end of the

park, and you can see the stadium from most vantage points. Some of the best views are from the elevated terrace area, near to the bandstand. One night in April 1941, Luftwaffe bombs fell in Leazes Park, landing right here by the bandstand, just a hundred yards or so from SJP. The Leazes End roof was damaged by shrapnel.

Back in 1892, the newly-named Newcastle United played its first match under that moniker at SJP on 24 December – a friendly against Middlesbrough, which United won 2-1. 'The goalkeeping on both sides was the feature of the match,' said one report.

The club's first really high-profile match under its new name was played at SJP on New Year's Day 1893 against the famous amateur side Corinthians. The tourists had been one of the greatest teams of the era, although their strictly amateur status had prevented them from entering or winning any competitions. Inevitably, the progress of the professional game had overtaken the amateurs. Newspapers said this latest Corinthians team was 'certainly the weakest which has ever visited Newcastle'. In a 'very one-sided game', United gave the amateurs an absolute thrashing. The *Sheffield Daily Telegraph* said Corinthians had 'smug satisfaction in their own prowess', and said 'the Tynesiders, just to show that football can be played in the north, waltzed round the team pitted against them by eight goals to one.'

The big score-line was somewhat more impressive than the sorry attendance figure of just 1,500, despite the apparent draw of the opposition, and the fact that the match was played on a public holiday. A layer of snow may have kept some fans away, but subsequent matches proved that this new 'united' club couldn't attract sufficient crowds. Newcastle were now in real financial trouble and the only possible solution was to gain membership of the elite group that was the Football League. Regular fixtures against a high standard of opposition should increase revenue, club officials believed.

So Newcastle applied for election to the Football League, and were invited to join the second division for the 1893/94 season, alongside fellow newcomers Woolwich Arsenal, Liverpool and Middlesbrough Ironopolis. This wasn't ideal. The playing standard and attendance figures for the second division weren't much higher than those in the Northern League, but it was one step closer to the first division, which was the summit that every club aspired to reach.

United's first Football League match was against Woolwich Arsenal, at the Manor Ground in Plumstead on 4 September 1893. Arsenal were London's first professional club, and there was plenty of interest from within the capital. Thousands of spectators were packed onto banked terraces that had been built up with heaps of rubbish, attracting flies from the surrounding marshes. Despite this apparent unpleasantness, it was a grand occasion. A contemporary sketch made at the match shows a packed crowd wearing top hats and boaters. One Arsenal fan has a supporter's card saying 'Play Up Reds!' pushed into his hatband. A group of fans, who have climbed a wall at the edge of the ground, are described in a caption as 'a few dead heads'.

Both teams' first-choice kit consisted of red shirts and white knickers, and the illustration seems to show

Newcastle playing in a change kit of black and white stripes (although one contemporary report says Newcastle played in *blue* and white). It also shows a couple of amusing incidents – a stray ball knocking a policeman's helmet off, and then another smashing a changing hut window. ('Glazier wanted!' says the caption.)

The game proved to be a tough introduction to league football. Newcastle were a goal down at half-time, and then went two down in the second half – with strong claims of handball dismissed by the referee. However, they eventually found their feet, and managed to come back to draw 2-2. Tom Crate scored the club's first league goal, and Jock Sorley scored the equaliser.

This was Sorley's last game for the club. He'd been a regular since the East End days, but he quit after an argument over wages, and moved to Blackburn Rovers. Cash-strapped Newcastle had asked Sorley and his colleagues to take a pay cut. Things were so tight for the league newcomers that they only managed the long journey to Plumstead thanks to a benevolent director footing the bill out of his own pocket.

After the match, a newspaper reporter interviewed Newcastle captain Willie Graham, discovering the 'thickset' Scottish centre-half 'in the midst of a team of towels, shower baths and wash-tubs'. Graham had played (alongside his brother Johnny) in the famous Preston North End 'Invincibles' team that won the inaugural Football League title in 1888/89. He'd joined Newcastle in 1892, while it was still playing as East End, and was an influential figure as the club began life at St James' Park and entered the Football League. His exchange with the reporter was published in the *Kentish Independent*.

'You look done up, Mr Graham,' said the reporter, meaning exhausted or 'done in'.

'So would you if you'd been travelling all night in a confounded train!' replied Graham.

'What did you think of the game?'

'We were terribly unlucky to draw. The second goal of the Arsenal was a fraud.'

'Then you think the referee incompetent?'

'I dare say he did his best,' said Graham. 'But I suppose you noticed that all our fellows appealed for hands and stood still.'

'What do you think of the Arsenal team?'

'Spanking good, indeed. They gave us as hard a game as we've ever had. Yet I think that when we get them up in the north we shall prove at least four goals their superior. That's merely my opinion.' It turned out to be a very perceptive opinion.

Arsenal made the return journey a few weeks later for what was the first league match played here at St James' Park. Just as Graham had predicted, Newcastle were superior from the kick-off, thrashing their opponents 6-0, with Joe Wallace and Willie Thompson both scoring hat-tricks. Thompson, one of the club's earliest high-scoring local centre-forwards (in the years before shirt numbering allowed them to be called 'number nines') scored 65 goals in 135 games for United.

But league football didn't pull in the crowds that Newcastle's directors had hoped for. This ground, still relatively small though it then was, was hardly bursting at the seams as only 2,000 turned up for the Arsenal match. There was clearly still a great deal of apathy among former East End and West End fans for the Newcastle United club. Cup matches were better attended. 7,000 saw United beat first division Sheffield Wednesday (then known simply as The Wednesday) in the FA Cup in January 1894, and 10,000 saw the home side get knocked out by Bolton Wanderers in February. High-profile opposition was obviously the key to drawing crowds, so the aim had to be to reach the first division as quickly as possible.

Continuing my wander around SJP, Barrack Road, to the west of the ground, takes its name from the main army barracks that were built here in the early 1800s. There were a good few pubs along Barrack Road at the time the football ground was first developed, including the Black Bull (which still exists on the same site today), the Duke of Wellington, the Windsor Hotel, the Bay Horse, and the Lord Hill, which was owned by club director John Black. In more recent years, the Magpie supporters' social club stood on the former site of the Lord Hill. And just down from there was the Tyne Brewery, which was opened in 1884, and was the home of Newcastle Brown Ale until the site was closed in 2005.

The Tyne Brewery was owned by John Barras who, in 1890, joined forces with four other local brewers to form the Newcastle Breweries company. To signify the coming together of the five brewers, Newcastle Breweries adopted a five-pointed blue star logo, which became closely associated with Newcastle United. The team wore a blue star on the front of their shirts for much of the 1980s and 1990s. Supporters of that vintage will clearly remember the air around the ground being thick with the smell of the brewery, adding to the heady atmosphere. The brewery is gone now, flattened, and undergoing redevelopment into a world-class science centre, in conjunction with Newcastle University. Newly-built on the brewery site nearest to Barrack Road is the university's huge and impressively shiny Business School building.

At the south west corner of the ground stands a statue in honour of Sir Bobby Robson, the former Newcastle manager, who died in 2009. Crafted in bronze by local sculptor Tom Maley, the statue stands almost 10 feet tall, and depicts Sir Bobby standing hands-in-pockets, with one foot on a football, gazing mindfully over fans entering the stadium grounds. This was a man who understood what the history and legacy of Newcastle United meant. 'What is a club in any case?' and all that.

Certainly the wander around St James' helps provide a better understanding of the foundations on which the club was built. Having been formed in 1881, it had been rehoused and renamed in 1892, and had entered the Football League in 1893, but there was still a long way to go before this club would resemble the one we know today. To find out what happened next, we need to walk past Sir Bobby towards the stadium reception for a look inside SJP.

East End supporters' 'Play Up' cards, from WN Sharpe c.1892
Left to right: Harry Jeffrey, Bobby Creilly and David Whitton

Inside St James' Park, groundstaff work on the pitch under the
Milburn and John Hall stands' 15 storey-high cantilever roof

Newcastle United team photo postcard, 1895
In playing kit, left to right; back row: Willie McKay, John
Henderson, Jimmy Stott; middle: (kneeling) James Collins, Bob
McDermid, Bob Foyers, Willie Miller, Willie Graham, (kneeling)
Willie Wardrope; front: Willie Thompson, Andy Aitken

5

A City United

St James' Park is very familiar to Newcastle fans, but there are a few treats hidden within its stands that many never see. The first thing to do is to take the elevator up to the second level and 'Cafe @ St James" (which could more accurately be called 'Coffee Machine @ St James"), where there is a row of cabinets that is as close as the club gets these days to having an official museum.

Among the photos and shirts are a few relics of the formative years of St James' and Newcastle United, including some fantastic East End supporters' cards, and it's worth a look. The supporters' cards are colourful little shields that were collected by kids and worn by adults – pushed into hat bands to demonstrate their support. The cards on display here, which must date from just before the 1892 name change, bear supporters' slogans like 'Play up East End!', 'Well played!' and 'Well done!' Known as 'Play Up' cards, they were manufactured by WN Sharpe, and sold in packs of six for a ha'penny.

The cards in this cabinet feature sketches depicting East End stars David Whitton, Harry Jeffrey and Bobby Creilly, all of whom continued to star for the club after it became Newcastle United. Whitton is pictured wearing a white cap, and all three players wear the club's red shirts. Local lad Whitton was a small but athletic keeper who kept goal for East End and Newcastle United throughout the 1892/93 season. Jeffrey, another Geordie lad, was a full-back and a regular in the Newcastle side that established itself in the Football League, until he sustained a bad injury during a match against Woolwich Arsenal in 1895 that ended his career, aged just 28.

Scots-born Creilly was a formidable jug-eared half-back who helped United get a foothold in the Football League, and played a key role in many of the club's formative games. Sadly, after football he fell into a life of destitution and mental illness. He was last heard of at the Newcastle City Lunatic Asylum in Coxlodge, now the St Nicholas Hospital. History can't even agree on how to spell his name. Wikipedia says 'Crielly', but this football card says 'Creilly', so let's go with that.

Also on display in these cabinets are fixture cards from the early 1900s, issued with the compliments of United players Andy Aitken and Alec Gardner, inviting fans to join them after the match in the respective pubs they ran – the Douglas Hotel and the Dun Cow. Scottish half-back Aitken captained United and his country in the first few years of the Edwardian period. Right-half Gardner, another Scot, succeeded Aitken as Newcastle captain. It's wonderful to see these items that can provide a link, however distant, to great players of the past that we were never able to see play.

The shift to St James' Park and election to the Football League placed the club at the centre of the city and gave it a unique representative role. Previously, it had represented the relatively small communities of Byker and Heaton, but now it was representing an entire city of 200,000 people. Excluding the odd friendly or cup match, the club had only played against other North East teams. But now they would play regularly against teams from the North West, from Yorkshire, from the West Midlands, and from London. The club was representing Newcastle on a national stage, at a time when few people outside of the North East had any idea of what went on in the city, other than a vague idea that it had some involvement in shipping coal.

William Clark Russell was a New York-born journalist for the *Newcastle Daily Chronicle* and the national *Daily Telegraph*. A former merchant seaman, he was very well-travelled, and wrote about the various places he'd visited. He loved Newcastle, and profiled the city for the *Telegraph* in the 1880s. 'I know of no spectacle in its way more stirring and impressive than the scene of the River Tyne as surveyed from the High Level Bridge,' he wrote. But few outsiders shared his passion for the city.

'I am afraid that the Tynesider's belief that the people who live in the South and West of England know little or nothing of the greatness and wealth of the district is only too well founded,' wrote Russell. 'What idea have the south-country people of the Tyne? The truth is, any object nearly three hundred miles distant is not only entirely out of range of metropolitan sympathy, but pretty nearly out of the confines of metropolitan knowledge. To hundreds and thousands the Tyne is barely a sound; it conveys no ideas.'

This wasn't just a symptom of a north-south divide. Newcastle was isolated from most of the rest of the country, in terms of location and popular thinking, and viewed by many as a remote and desolate backwater. (Some might say that view remains prevalent today.) But football was an increasingly popular sport with increasingly widespread coverage. Newcastle's exploits on the football field would be featured in newspapers around the country. Reporters would come here, as would visiting teams and supporters. And United would travel to foreign towns as ambassadors for their great northern city.

'Local patriotism runs extraordinarily high here, and the man who should venture to hint to a Newcastle audience that their "canny toon" is not quite the marvellous idealism of streets and houses they think it, would need an uncommonly bold and adventurous spirit,' wrote Russell. 'It is difficult to understand why this local devotion should be marked here to a degree not to be found in any other town in Great Britain. But it is so. And what finer race of people shall you find in other parts of this kingdom? They are the warmest-hearted people in the world, and of such a people and of such a town they have built among them, one cannot hear too much, nor feel too hearty an admiration.'

Geordie cheeks may have blushed at Mr Russell's flattery, but it's interesting that an outsider should pick up on local patriotism and devotion to the 'canny toon' at a time when the football club was establishing itself. It was early days, but the people of Newcastle would come to embrace the club with the same pride and passion they had for their city.

We're now heading up the steps into the main reception, for a behind-the-scenes glimpse at St James' Park. This is where the players walk, having disembarked from their coach, wrapped in oversized headphones and clutching bootbags, past cheering fans and peering TV cameras, into reception, through the corridor, and out to the changing rooms and the tunnel leading down to the pitch. Opposite the tunnel is the sponsors' backdrop used for post-match TV interviews. The media centre is nearby, with its press conference stage, and facilities for the journalists to have their lunch and plug in their laptops.

The home and away changing rooms could hardly be more different. The away facilities are remarkably basic, but the home changing room provides everything the modern footballer might need – even an overhead locker with a personal safe in which to store their diamond-encrusted earrings. There's a treatment table in the middle of the room, and a water dispenser and fridge full of Lucozade Sport in the corner. Off to the side of the changing room are showers and an ice bath. There are still clods of mud on the floor from the weekend's match, and flipcharts are lying around showing marking responsibilities for corners and free-kicks. There's a sign reminding the players to stay hydrated. 'If you're thirsty, it's too late!' The clock on the wall isn't working, stuck at a crucial time for match preparation – five to three. Is that a deliberate ruse to keep the players on their toes?

Back in the early 1890s, the players didn't have a changing room. They'd pull on their heavy shirts and long, baggy knickers, rub their legs with liniment, and strap on their shin-pads in the Lord Hill pub on Barrack Road. (The away team would change in adjacent pubs, or at the County Hotel by the train station, or otherwise travel to the match by train and brake already kitted up.)

When St James' did eventually get a changing room, it was burgled. The *Chronicle* reported in November 1898 that the SJP dressing room had been broken into on a Friday night, and 'a quantity of training apparatus', including two 'punching balls' used by the players on a daily basis, had been stolen. 'In future,' the paper reported, 'the public will not be admitted to the ground except on practice and match days.'

Outside of the changing rooms, we can wander down the players' tunnel, under the 'Howay the Lads' sign, and then up a few steps into the daylight and out to the hallowed pitch. The playing surface looks magnificent, like dew-covered baize, but that wasn't always the case. From the very earliest days, even before East End moved here, there were complaints about the St James' Park pitch. It was regarded as one of the worst in the region – and in the country.

'The West End ground is most unsuitable to football,' reported the *Northern Echo* in November 1888, 'and remembering the high reputation of the club, we were astonished to see it. Between goal and goal there is a most pronounced dip, and on Saturday the goal mouth at the bottom end, for some 20 yards out, was nothing but a greasy, muddy slope of the most treacherous nature.'

It didn't change much under East End or during the early days of Newcastle United. The football writer Henry Leach said that footballers did not mind playing away matches, 'except in the case of Newcastle United, the ground of which the ancient Britons might have thought good for football, but which the modern artist always dreams of in his worst nightmares.'

Things have improved greatly, but not entirely, since then. Although efforts have been made over the years to level the pitch, a visible slope still exists. By all accounts there's a gentleman's agreement still in place between club captains that, whoever wins the coin toss, Newcastle will always be allowed to kick 'downhill' towards the Gallowgate end in the second half. However, if such an agreement exists, many opposition captains don't seem to be aware of it.

Standing this close to the pitch is a thrilling experience for a Newcastle United devotee. The heart beats a little faster, and there are proverbial butterflies in the stomach. This is, of course, just about the nearest most of us will ever get to playing for our club. And then a look up and around at the vast stadium that encloses the pitch. We're sheltered from the noise of the city and, but for a couple of birds flapping their wings and rising into the sky, the place is entirely still. It's a quiet and magnificent place to be.

Next is a walk up into the stands to sit in the best seat in the house – the one used by the club's owner. It's a much comfier seat than most fans are used to, and it would be really quite pleasant to sit here all day, soaking in the unique ambience of this stadium, completely empty yet full of atmosphere. Weirdly, within the silence there's an odd sense of being able to hear crowd noise. Those hairs on the back of the neck are at it again. It's possible that memories are being triggered in the back of the mind. Or perhaps this place has absorbed something from the hundreds of thousands of folk who've passed through here over the past 130-plus years, their passion and noise recorded somehow for the ages within the concrete and steel.

This is just one of 52,409 seats in this stadium, making St James' Park the fourth biggest football ground in England after Wembley, Old Trafford and the Emirates. Without doubt, SJP is one of the key factors that makes Newcastle United a special club. The stadium's city centre location isn't unique among other big clubs, although an increasing number are moving to newbuild grounds, sometimes away from their traditional fan bases, often in soulless out-of-town locations. Since it has been Newcastle United, this club has never left its home, and the sense of history that exists here is palpable. (There is also the small matter of fact that SJP is located in the greatest city on the world.)

Recalling visits to other major football grounds in England, while trying desperately to avoid bias, it's difficult to think of any that can compare with SJP for location, for impact, for majesty. Away fans must feel this too, whether they arrive via the A1, past the Angel of the North, across the Redheugh Bridge, or by train, walking out of Central Station, up Pink Lane. There it is, looming over the city, a stunning monument to the greatest game. It's a sight that generates great excitement and one clear thought – *this* is football.

It's a towering structure, this place. The Milburn and Leazes stands have seven levels, and from the top you can look out over the city and for miles beyond – towards Byker and the birthplace of Stanley FC. These upper levels were added in 1998, one of several major redevelopments that have transformed the stadium since the 1880s. It's fascinating to wonder what those who played and spectated at SJP in its earliest days would make of the stadium now.

When East End moved to SJP in 1892, they dismantled the Heaton Junction pavilion and took it with them. That small timber enclosure provided shelter for a few hundred fans, but the majority would stand in the open on muddy banks. SJP's first proper stand was built along the west side of the pitch in the late 1890s, and further enclosures increased the capacity to more than 30,000 by the turn of the 20th century. In 1905 a new West Stand was built, and the terrace enclosures helped to double the capacity to 60,000. The Leazes End was covered in 1929, and floodlights were erected in the early 1950s. The East Stand, which still remains, was added in 1973. The timber West Stand was demolished in 1987, having stood for 82 years, and was replaced by a new stand named after Jackie Milburn. New Gallowgate and Leazes Stands were added in the mid-1990s, with the standing terraces removed.

Behind the stands, much of St James' Park is now dedicated to corporate use and hospitality, and there are scores of meeting and conference rooms, banqueting and function suites, including Club 206, dedicated to Alan Shearer and his 206 goals in the Newcastle number nine shirt. Private boxes overlook the pitch along the length of the Milburn Stand (Shearer's is called 'Wor Box') and there are TV studios in the north-west corner.

The commercialisation of SJP can't be ignored, and multiple adverts are visible around the pitch and throughout the seating areas. The ground's first advertising hoarding was paid for in the early 1890s by club director John Black to promote his afore-mentioned Lord Hill pub. The Lord Hill was a popular haunt of Newcastle players, and it was reported that some of the players would have a couple of pre-match drinks while changing into their kit there. Arthur Appleton, in *Hotbed of Soccer*, tells the tale of an unnamed defender who, having enjoyed the Lord Hill's pre-match hospitality, was forced to ask a teammate, after the game had started, 'Which way wi' kickin'?'

Perhaps the pre-match drinks did have a negative effect on the players' game. After finishing fourth in their first season in the second division, Newcastle really began to struggle. 1894/95 saw some terrible defeats, including 9-0 to Burton Wanderers in the league, and 7-1 to Aston Villa in the FA Cup. Those two scorelines remain Newcastle biggest defeats in those competitions to this day.

The Burton Wanderers result was particularly embarrassing. The opposition club, from Burton upon Trent, no longer exists, but at the time it was a fellow second division club. Newcastle had just comfortably beaten Newton Heath, the club that would become Manchester United, 3-0. However, just as that game was about to kick off, captain Willie Graham received a telegram advising him that his father had been killed. He headed home to Scotland, and missed the Burton game. His teammates seemed to be affected by Graham's tragedy, and certainly missed his presence in the middle of the field. Burton scored 'almost immediately', and were 4-0 up at half-time. Five more goals followed in the second half as, according to the *London Standard*, they 'made a sorry example of Newcastle United'. Brothers Arthur and Ade Capes scored three and four goals respectively for Burton.

Newcastle were struggling financially, too, to the extent that they were sometimes unable to pay visiting clubs their share of the gate money, and a debt-clearing benefit match had to be arranged – against unlikely benefactors Sunderland. (Newcastle enjoyed the profits from a 6,000-strong gate, but didn't enjoy the match – they lost 3-1.)

Not for the first – or last – time, the club was in crisis. A public meeting was called, at which it was decided that big changes were needed if Newcastle United were going to survive. Those present agreed to pursue 'a policy of revival'. Investment was required in order to improve the playing staff and the ground, so a new set of ten shilling shares was issued. The people of Newcastle faced a choice – back your football club or lose it. In a demonstration of the early bond the city had with the game, the shares were quickly and enthusiastically snapped up.

In the summer of 1895, the club brought in almost an entire team's worth of new players, including tricky little forward Willie Wardrope, and the brilliant and influential half-back Andy Aitken. Wardrope scored 22 goals in his first season for Newcastle, while Aitken hit 12 from midfield. Aitken would go on to captain the club, and lead it to previously-unknown highs. His was undoubtedly one of the most important signings in Newcastle's history. But there was also another very significant new arrival at the club, and he wasn't a player.

Frank G Watt was a former joiner who had become a respected football figure in Scotland, where he'd worked as a referee and administrator. He was known for his keen eye for a player, and had gained a strong reputation as a team-builder. He was working as the secretary of Dundee FC when Newcastle's directors wrote to him asking if he could recommend a secretary for their club. Watt did recommend someone, Willie Waugh of the St Bernard's club. But Newcastle wrote back to him: 'Why not take the job yourself, Frank?' After some persuasion from the Newcastle committee, he eventually agreed, and the 41-year-old Scot began a 36-year-long career at Newcastle, during which he transformed the club from a struggling second division side to the best team in Edwardian England.

There's no way to underestimate the impact that Watt had on Newcastle United, almost from the moment he walked through the door. He built a new team, implemented new tactics and training regimes, renovated the ground and facilities, reorganised the club's administration, reinvigorated its income, stoked enthusiasm among supporters, and brought ever-increasing crowds to St James' Park.

'A fresh wave of enthusiasm swept over the town,' wrote JH Morrison in *The Book of Football*, published in 1905. 'Football in Newcastle had at length emerged from the chrysalis stage. Mr Watt certainly had a very long row to hoe, but efficient management ran hand-in-hand with increased public support, and, whenever the funds permitted, investments were made in ground and team improvements.'

There was one further major development in 1895. The club's name change to Newcastle United had never been legally registered. In December 1895 the East End Football Company Limited officially changed its name to Newcastle United Football Club Limited. Now the club really was 'United'.

Back in the present, in the peaceful surrounds of an empty St James' Park, it seems amazing that this place could ever be taken for granted. A proper look around and a delve into its history provides plenty of reminders of how important SJP is to the club, its supporters, and its city. It's clear that this great stadium, in all of its incarnations, has been a key factor in Newcastle United's success and standing in the world of football. There really is no place like home.

Frank Watt
Newcastle United secretary / manager

Robert Sinclair's Newcastle United cigarette cards, c.1898
The first set of NUFC club cards, produced by Newcastle
tobacconist Sinclair. Left to right: Andy Aitken, Willie
Wardrope, Joe Ro(d)gers, Matt Kingsley

Newcastle United team postcard 1897-1898
*The team that won promotion to the first division. In playing
kit, left to right; back row: Tommy Ghee, John White, Jack
Ostler, Jimmy Stott; middle: Charlie Watts, Jimmy Jackson,
Malcolm Lennox, Willie G Stewart; front: Ron Allan, Johnny
Harvey, Johnnie Campbell, Andy Aitken, Willie Wardrope. Also
pictured are Frank Watt, trainer Tommy Dodds and
groundsman Mr Cockburn*

6

Black and White

On the first floor of the NUFC club shop, underneath the Gallowgate stand at St James' Park, there are two framed replica shirts. The first is a long-sleeved, crew-necked Cambridge blue shirt. The second is also long-sleeved, but has collars, and is bright red. Both are embroidered with a modern badge stating: 'Newcastle United: Founded in 1881'.

These shirts are interesting for two reasons. The first is that the club has always, as far as I can recall, promoted the fact that Newcastle United was founded in 1892. But there was life in this football club before then, and it's good to see that acknowledged. The second interesting thing about these shirts is much more obvious: they aren't black and white.

If I'm honest, I'm not a regular visitor to the club shop, but I've ducked inside today to shelter from a sudden storm. Through the windows a passing pedestrian is being lashed by sideways rain that's whipped along by a whistling wind. A handful of blokes have sought shelter in here, browsing the racks in wet cagoules, one of them whistling along to the song that's playing over the shop's sound system.

Just inside the main entrance there's a range of football kits from around the world, a nicely cosmopolitan touch – although it seems unlikely that many Newcastle fans will be buying the prominently-displayed red and white-striped Atletico Madrid shirt. The rest of the shop is, of course, dedicated to NUFC merchandise, including replica kits of the home, away, goalkeeper and seemingly pointless third/European variety. There is also all manner of training kit, with racks and racks of t-shirts, shorts, sweatshirts, sweatpants, tracksuits and pretty much anything else a football fan seeking to emulate his or her heroes could want.

There's some odd stuff here, too. There are spray tattoos, inflatable chairs and stuffed monkeys in NUFC pyjamas. There are NUFC Pez dispensers, nodding dogs and Toon Army toilet seats. For wacky stag do types there are NUFC jester hats and 'second skin' black and white-striped full-body leotards. And then there is the 'NUFC Onesie', which is essentially a black and white babygrow for fully-grown adults.

All of that is downstairs. Upstairs there is more replica kit and other black and white merchandise – and also the NUFC ticket office. That seems a very clever move on behalf of the club in terms of getting fans into the shop. (Want to buy a ticket for Saturday's match? Right this way, sir, and would you like an NUFC travel mug with that?) And it's upstairs that you can find the blue and red replica shirts. Which brings us back to the main point: Newcastle United haven't always worn black and white.

As we've already seen, there doesn't seem to be any

record of the colours initially worn by Stanley FC, but after Stanley changed its name to East End, from at least 1883, we know that the club wore blue jerseys and white knickerbockers. The original long-sleeved jerseys were most likely fairly heavy knitted affairs, and the 'knickers' were baggy knee-length trousers that would have been held up with a belt. East End's kit did occasionally vary, and for the 1885/86 season the club wore blue shirts with one orange vertical stripe sewn on – a design revisited by Adidas for a Newcastle away kit to a mixed reception in 1997/98.

So East End weren't playing in black and white, and neither were their cross-town rivals West End. The West Enders played in red and black hooped shirts, and then, after setting up home at St James' Park, in red and black halved shirts. Or at least they *probably* played in red and black. It's difficult to pinpoint exact colours and shades as none of the kits survive, and obviously the few photos that exist aren't in colour. Adidas designers interpreted West End's hooped shirt as maroon and blue for another away shirt homage in 1995/96.

For East End, there was a major change in 1890, with the club switching to play in – horror of horrors – red and white. The new kit consisted of red jerseys and white knickers, and was in use when the club moved to St James' Park and changed its name to Newcastle United. So it's a fact that Newcastle United played in red and white before they played in black and white. As the replica in the shop shows, however, Newcastle's shirts were solid red, unlike those of Sunderland, who played in red and white-striped jerseys and black knickers from around 1888.

Newcastle's time in red and white didn't last long, and club shop-goers certainly seem to much prefer the current colours – the famous black and white. The switch to black and white was precipitated by the election of the club to the Football League. Under league rules, clubs were supposed to register different colours, but Newcastle played their first league season in red and white – causing multiple kit clashes. For instance, in their very first league match, against the red-shirted Woolwich Arsenal in 1893, Newcastle were required to wear a change kit – which just happened to be black and white.

There was also another simmering problem, namely dissatisfaction among supporters of the uprooted East End and the defunct West End that had prompted the name change to Newcastle United. The perceived 'merger' was understandably unpopular with some, and the fact that Newcastle United played in the same colours as East End couldn't have helped. A change was required, and in August 1894 the decision was taken, as the minutes from a club meeting reveal: 'It was agreed that the Club's colours should be changed from red shirts and white knickers to black and white shirts (two inch stripe) and dark knickers.'

Those 'dark knickers' may originally have been black or grey, but were more commonly blue. It wasn't until the 1920s that the club eventually settled on black shorts. The stockings, some say socks, were black, and have pretty much remained so, barring several ill-fated dalliances with 'unlucky' white.

Newcastle weren't the first club to wear black and

white stripes. Notts County, the world's oldest professional club, wore black and white from around 1890. (County were in the second division alongside Newcastle in 1894/95, so that's at least one kit clash that wasn't avoided.) Juventus, the Old Lady of Italian football, began wearing black and white stripes in 1903 due to a connection with Notts County via player John Savage. Grimsby Town started wearing the black and white around 1909. Dunfermline Athletic adopted the colours around the same time. But the earliest club to play in black and white stripes was probably St Mirren, who were wearing them from around 1884.

So why did Newcastle United decide on black and white stripes? There are several theories. One of them harks back to the English Civil War, and to the first Duke of Newcastle, William Cavendish, and his Whitecoats regiment, who wore overcoats made from undyed sheep's wool (which is black as well as white). They fought under the Cavendish heraldic crest, which features three white stag heads on a black shield. Cavendish and his regiment were local heroes, and the story goes that NUFC chose black and white stripes in their honour.

Another theory involves Dominican friars, who wore black and white robes, and have also long been associated with Newcastle. Blackfriars, just south of St James' Park near what is now Chinatown, is a Dominican Friary dating back to the 13th century. One particular Friar, a Dutchman named Dalmatius Houtmann, was apparently a very keen Newcastle United fan, and was friendly with the club's directors. Could he have had something to do with the switch to black and white?

A third theory involves a pair of magpies that apparently nested in a St James' Park stand and were 'adopted' by the Newcastle players. It's a romantic idea, but it's far more likely that the club's association with magpies began after – and because of – the switch to black and white. All three theories are interesting, but unnecessarily complicated. The real reason Newcastle United play in black and white stripes is much simpler.

It was all to do with necessity. The club had to change colours to avoid kit clashes. Football kits were expensive to buy, and it wasn't uncommon in the Victorian era for clubs to share them. And there happened to be a black and white-striped kit available – the one used by the Northumberland FA county side.

We know Northumberland wore black and white stripes when they played at St James' in 1887 – and they had probably played in black and white for several years previous to that, with the Association having been founded back in 1883. We also know that East End – and subsequently Newcastle United – borrowed the Northumberland strips whenever they needed a change kit. Indeed, in *Hotbed of Soccer*, Arthur Appleton says that East End 'played in red, with their alternative strip the county jerseys of black and white stripes'.

Newcastle, of course, was the traditional county town of Northumberland (and remained a part of Northumberland until the county of Tyne and Wear was created in 1974). And it just so happens that the county of Northumberland has an official tartan, a checked pattern known as Shepherd Plaid. And Shepherd Plaid happens to be black and white. It's closely linked to the Percys, the powerful family that held the Dukedom of Northumberland, and is made – like Cavendish's white coats – using undyed black and white sheep's wool.

Fragments of the Plaid have been found that date back to the third century AD, meaning it was worn when the Romans were here. The Romans founded Newcastle as a settlement called Pons Aelius, or Aelian Bridge, named for Emperor Hadrian. So there has been a link between Newcastle and Shepherd Plaid since the very earliest days of the city. In summary, Newcastle has always been associated with black and white. They've long been established as the colours that unite this club, its city, and the Geordie nation.

Should we, at this point, tackle the thorny issue of the origin of the term 'Geordie'? Again, there are several differing theories. The two most likely of these date back to the 18th century. The first is that, during the Jacobite Rebellion of 1745, the people of Newcastle supported George II and were subsequently labelled 'Geordies', probably as a term of abuse by those who were against the Hanoverian king. However, there doesn't seem to be any reliable evidence to support this theory.

The second theory is that, from the late 1700s, the word 'Geordie' (or 'Geordy') was used to describe North East pitmen, simply because there were a lot of North East pitmen called George. The best source of evidence for this second theory is John Trotter Brockett's snappily-titled 1829 book *A Glossary of North Country Words in Use with Their Etymology and Affinity to Other Languages; and Occasional Notices of Local Customs and Popular Superstitions.* It contains the entry: 'GEORDIE, George – a very common

name among the pitmen. "How! Geordie man! how is't?'"
Also, from the early 1800s, these local pitmen used
George Stephenson's safety lamp, which they nicknamed
the 'Geordie lamp'.

The modern meaning of 'Geordie' is also subject to
differing definitions. You no longer need to work down a
pit to be a Geordie, but you do need to come from Tyneside, or live within sight of the Tyne, or have been born
with a ham and pease pudding stottie in your gob, suck-
led on Brown Ale, and recited as your first words the
entire original lyrics of *Blaydon Races*. Certainly, 'Geordie'
can no longer refer to folk from the entire North East.
People from Sunderland ('Mackems') or Middlesbrough
('Smoggies') will at the very least grind their teeth with
mild irritation should they be referred to as 'Geordies'.
That's certainly got something to do with footballing
rivalry because, regardless of where they were born or
live, 'Geordies' are also supporters of Newcastle United.

The latest black and white home shirt is prominently displayed all around the club shop. In the current era
of commercialisation, the shirt changes pretty much
every season. The black and white stripes remain, but
there are various design tweaks to the collar and sleeves,
with new sponsor logos, and various patches for league
and cup competitions. In recent years, the shirts have
featured a blank area on the back designed to encourage
fans to pay a bit more to get a number and name added,
the thinking obviously being that their shirts will look a
bit daft if they don't.

Of course there was no club shop back in the 1890s,
or any club merchandise to speak of. If you wanted to buy

football gear in Newcastle back then, your best bet was to try Henry A Murton's department store at the Monument. Murton's sold footballs and football kits, with newspaper ads promising 'a choice selection of every requisite. (Terms: prompt cash.)' Newcastle United used Murton's footballs, and the store also sponsored the official match programmes (basically postcards showing team line-ups and kick-off times) following the move to St James' Park.

The storm has passed, and the sun is shining on damp streets, so it's time to head out of the club shop and around the corner to St James' Street – the street that has so cruelly been shorn on its sign of its apostrophe. It's a row of mostly very handsome three-storey Georgian/Victorian townhouses, although the one we're looking for has been disappointingly uglified, with scratchy grey rendering pebble-dashed across its front façade. This is number three St James' Street, and it now occupies the end of the row, with the adjacent number one having been demolished to make way for a small car park.

Number three is now home to an insurance brokers, but back in the 1890s this was Frank Watt's home – and his office. It was here that the secretary extraordinaire plotted and planned the rise of Newcastle United. He also got the builders in. Unhappy with the players changing in the Lord Hill pub, he built a 'stripping room' in his backyard. There is still a red brick extension building visible at the back of the property. Now the players could change, cross the back lane, and enter St James' Park via the players' tunnel, then located at the Gallowgate end of the ground.

As secretary and treasurer, Watt was incredibly influential, but it was his ability as a team builder that was most evident to Newcastle supporters. In the days before managers or scouts, Watt effectively fulfilled both roles, scouring England – and particularly Scotland – for football's best talents. One major new signing was rangy centre-forward Jock Peddie, signed from Third Lanark for £135 after a friendly with the Glasgow club. Watt considered Peddie to have the fiercest shot he had ever seen. The Scot was Newcastle's top scorer for four consecutive seasons.

That was some achievement on Peddie's behalf, because another of Frank Watt's signings was one of the greatest goalscorers of the Victorian era, signed from one of the era's greatest clubs – Sunderland. Johnnie Campbell had won the league championship three times on Wearside, and had been the league's top scorer in all three seasons. Overall, he'd scored 136 goals in 186 games for Sunderland's 'Team of All Talents', assembled at great cost, mainly from north of the border, by brilliant former East End secretary Tom Watson.

Campbell swapped Wearside for Tyneside along with teammate Johnny Harvey (or Harvie), a little goal-scoring inside-right. Another 'Team of All Talents' star (and another Johnny), the teetotal John Auld, had already spent a season at Newcastle as football's first Wear-Tyne transfer, so Campbell and Harvey were following in famous footsteps.

Johnnie Campbell was the nearest thing football had to a superstar. Arthur Appleton says Campbell was 'as celebrated in his day as Hughie Gallacher was in his'. Yet he joined Newcastle for just £40, plus a £10 signing-on fee. Although he played only a single full season at Newcastle, seeing out the end of his career, he became a big crowd favourite. After retirement, he ran a pub on Barrack Road, the Darnell Hotel, which became a popular haunt for Newcastle fans.

The goals of Peddie, Campbell and Harvey helped power the club up the league, and attendances went up, too. In fact, they shot up, from an average of around 4,000 in 1894/95 to 7,000 in 1895/96, 8,000 in 1896/97, and almost 12,000 in 1897/98. In modern terms, we're now getting up towards Championship-level attendances. At one match that season, in December 1897, 24,000 spectators turned up at SJP to see Newcastle play Burnley, setting a second division record. Then finally, at the end of 1897/98, Newcastle won promotion to the first division.

As with anything involving Newcastle, promotion wasn't straightforward. The club finished in second place in their division and, with no automatic promotion on offer, went into a series of 'test match' play-offs, also involving first division bottom clubs Blackburn and Stoke, and second division champions Burnley. Going into the final play-off in April 1898, Newcastle needed to beat Blackburn at home and rely on either Stoke or Burnley to lose. SJP was rammed with a crowd of 16,000 fans. In fact, there were so many people inside the ground that a barrier collapsed, causing two young lads to be taken to hospital with broken legs. Backed by the big crowd, Newcastle despatched Blackburn 4-0.

Unfortunately, Stoke and Burnley played out a scandalous 0-0 draw in which there was not a single shot on goal. As neither team had lost, this meant Stoke would retain their place in the first division and Burnley would be promoted, while Blackburn would be relegated and Newcastle would remain in the second division. However, Blackburn and Newcastle joined together to protest the dastardly manner in which Stoke and Burnley had contrived their result. There was plenty of sympathy, from the press and from football legislators, and a few weeks later the Football League announced that the first division would be extended to accommodate wronged clubs Blackburn and Newcastle, and that the 'test match' system would be scrapped. Newcastle United had finally arrived in the big time.

The club prepared for life in the first division by making more new signings, including goalkeeper Matt Kingsley, who the *Journal* said was a 'stalwart and muscular footballer', and right-winger Joe Rogers, who had 'rare sprinting and dribbling powers'. Kingsley would become the club's first official international player, while Rogers would become its first 'unofficial' international, but more of that later.

In the meantime, the club erected a 'commodious' new timber stand at the Barrack Road side of the ground, built a new standing embankment on the Leazes Terrace side, and surrounded the pitch with a new 'substantial' rail. 'The whole of the appointments have been carried out so as to ensure the comfort and convenience, as well as the safety, of the public,' said the *Journal*.

The ground improvement work wasn't uniformly

popular. The residents of Leazes Terrace protested, and launched an appeal with the city council claiming that United were in breach of the conditions of the ground's lease. At a council meeting, Alderman Thomas Richardson raised a motion, stating that he had no problem with football or footballers, but that the youth of the city should have free access to the Town Moor and Castle Leazes. They could not gain free access to the area known as St James' Park, he said, because it was enclosed, and operated by individuals 'who cared nothing whatever for sport, but whose sole object was to make money... which was contrary to their lease.'

According to the *Newcastle Courant*, Alderman Richardson said that the company that held the lease was 'largely composed of publicans and others interested in the liquor traffic'. He described the 'raising of a huge mound in front of Leazes Terrace', and the erection of walls and enclosures, all done on an agricultural lease. 'Not only had the residents of Leazes Terrace to complain of the row, but they had to complain that the mound blocked their view.'

Gate money was taken at the ground, the Alderman said, and two particular matches had generated profits of £500 and £700 respectively – huge sums at the time. 'The men who used the ground were paid players, and the whole business was one solely for making money,' he said. The reputation of the council was at stake, and they should set an example by 'seeing that the covenants in their leases were strictly observed'. But the Alderman's fellow councillors must have been Newcastle United fans: his motion was defeated by 37 to 5.

That was a substantial victory for Newcastle United, but, as they began life in the first division, further victories would be harder to come by.

Jock Peddie (Wills Football Series, c.1902) and Alec Gardner (Cohen Weenen Football Captains, c.1907) cigarette cards

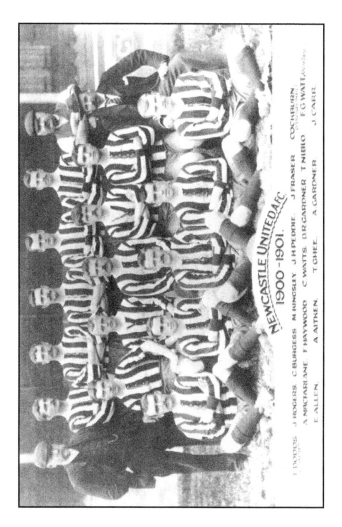

Newcastle United team postcard 1900-1901
This team finished sixth in the first division. In kit, left to right;
back row: Joe Rogers, Charles Burgess, Matt Kingsley, Jock
Peddie, John Fraser; middle: Alex Macfarlane, Fred Heywood,
Charlie Watts, Dave Gardner, Tom Niblo; front: Edward Allen,
Andy Aitken, Tommy Ghee, Alec Gardner, Jack Carr

7

The Magpies

As Newcastle United head towards the 20th century, I'm heading towards a football memorabilia exhibition at the city's excellent Discovery Museum. The museum is located in Blandford House, the grand former Co-operative Wholesale Society Headquarters at Blandford Square, just a short stroll away from St James' Park, down what was Blenheim Street, now renamed St James' Boulevard. The red-brick Co-op headquarters was built in 1899, as Newcastle United were establishing themselves as a first division club.

The first thing you see on entering the museum is the magnificent Turbinia, a 105-foot long turbine-powered steamship built by Charles Parsons at Wallsend in 1894. Nicknamed the 'Greyhound of the North Sea', it was by far the fastest ship of its time, able to power along at speeds of up to 34 knots or 40 miles per hour. Like the building it stands in, the Turbinia is another example of the remarkable things that were being created in Newcastle upon Tyne during the late Victorian period.

There's lots more to see here, including the permanent Newcastle Story and Story of the Tyne exhibitions, not to mention the Tyne & Wear Archives, which hold many of the newspapers and other sources utilised to write this book. But we're here for a temporary exhibition celebrating Newcastle United. Navigating past several hundred school kids in hi-visibility tabards, a wander around the exhibition reveals a plethora of football photos, shirts, programmes, ticket stubs, scarves, newspaper clippings and more, all supported by quotes from fans supplying their memories. Unsurprisingly, the eye is particularly drawn to the exhibition's earliest artefacts, from a time that no living fan can remember.

Newcastle's first few months in the first division, in the 1898/99 season, were extremely difficult. Despite the obvious talents of individuals like Matt Kingsley, Andy Aitken and Jock Peddie, the team's flaws were exposed in the opening game, at home to Wolverhampton Wanderers. 'As a team they lacked pace and finish in passing, and easily succumbed to the Wolves by four goals to two,' said the *Journal*. Peddie's two goals at least gave the big crowd something to cheer. 'Over 20,000 spectators were present,' said the paper, 'and, like good sportsmen, they warmly acknowledged the better play of the visitors.'

Newcastle went ten games without a win until, in November 1898, they surprisingly beat Liverpool 3-0, with Peddie scoring another two goals, in front of another 20,000-strong SJP crowd. 'A brilliant triumph for United!' trumpeted the *Journal*. The visit of Liverpool brought a return to Newcastle for their secretary Tom Watson, who the *Journal* said was 'one of the principle pioneers of the sport in the North of England.'

'A Tynesider bred and born, no one feels more proud

than Mr Tom Watson at the elevation of Newcastle United to the league,' commented the paper. 'But, like all supporters of the "magpie" colours, he is much disappointed at the present position of the club.' This was one of the earliest recorded references to magpies in relation to Newcastle United. And it indicates the origin of the famous nickname that endures today.

The city's original 'Magpies' were actually bicycle riders – the Newcastle Magpies was a popular local cycling club in the 1890s. This period was known as the 'golden age' of cycling, with the rudimentary penny farthing replaced by the much more accessible safety bicycle. Newcastle had already produced a cycling world champion, George Waller, who was born at Gallowgate, right next to the site of St James' Park. The sport became a full-on craze in the last decade of the 19th century, and there would have been hundreds of cyclists pedalling their way around Newcastle.

But within a few years of the football club adopting its black and white stripes, newspapers began referring to Newcastle United as 'the Magpies' in match reports. The magpie began to appear as a mascot, too, initially in newspaper cartoons, which would later pit Newcastle's black and white bird against Sunderland's black cat. Magpies subsequently appeared on club stationery, programmes, and even a couple of club crests, becoming indelibly linked with the club. Newcastle United are the Magpies, and the black and white birds have been associated with the club ever since.

Why magpies, though? That old theory about a pair of nesting birds rears its head again, but it seems pretty obvious that the club was nicknamed the Magpies simply because of its black and white shirts. There's an early Ogden's football card that depicts a suited and booted magpie holding a football under its wing. It states that Newcastle 'are known as the Magpies from their black and white-striped jerseys, and are also known as the Geordies'.

Magpies don't have a great reputation. They nick shiny things from humans and raid other birds' nests for eggs and chicks. But most notably for a mascot of a football club, they're associated with superstition. 'One for sorrow, two for joy, three for a girl, four for a boy,' and all that. An encounter with a single magpie is said to bring bad luck, unless you greet the bird ('Hello Mr Magpie!'), or salute it, or do something else that will make passers-by think you're nuts. The reason for this ill-fortune? Supposedly, when Jesus was on the cross, all of the birds in the world sang to comfort him – except for the magpie, who was cursed as a result.

Is that why Newcastle United never seem to win anything? Because of an unlucky mascot afflicted with a 2,000-year-old curse? You would have to think not. And, as the magpie is regarded as one of the most intelligent creatures on the planet (it can count, use tools, and imitate the human voice, and is one of the few species of animal – and the only non-mammal – able to recognise itself in a mirror), the magpie would probably agree with you.

Newcastle are by no means the only club nicknamed 'the Magpies', and plenty of other clubs that play in black and white share the moniker, including Notts County and

Alnwick Town, plus (deep breath) Maidenhead United in Berkshire, Dorchester Town in Dorset, Brimsdown Rovers (a former club of David Beckham) in North London, Alresford Town in Hampshire, Loxwood FC in West Sussex, Long Sutton Athletic in Lincolnshire, Penzance AFC in Cornwall, Dereham Town in Norfolk, Amersham Town in Buckinghamshire, Colney Heath in Hertfordshire, Stonehouse Town in Gloucestershire, Llanfyllin Town in Mid Wales, Barmouth and Dyffryn United in West Wales, Wakehurst FC in Northern Ireland, Rabat Ajax in Malta... and probably a whole load more. There's also a Spanish team called Magpie FC, or Urraca CF in the local lingo. They play in royal blue, so perhaps something has been lost in translation. (To be fair, a magpie's black feathers are glossed with a petroleum blue sheen, and the colour blue has also regularly turned up on Newcastle kits over the years.)

The magpie, then, provided a nickname and became a mascot for the club. Today, the club has two cheerleading magpie mascots, Monty and Maggie, who appear by the side of the SJP pitch on a match day, attempting to get kids big and small to clap and sing along with various songs. And for several heady years around the 1950s, the club's match day mascot was simply a bloke in black and white top hat and tails who walked around the cinder track ringing a bell and waving a brolly.

But back in the club's formative years, Newcastle United had another mascot – a black and white Great Dane named Rex. The dog was owned by Frank Watt, and would watch every match at St James' Park, being tied to railings by the pitch. Legend has it that Rex once escaped from his lead and attacked the opposition team. He appears prominently alongside the club's players and staff in team photos from the early 1900s – one of which is on display in a glass cabinet at this exhibition at the Discovery museum. Another (unnamed) dog owned by Watt appears on an earlier team photo, proving that the magpie wasn't the only animal associated with Newcastle United FC.

Frank Watt's signature can be found on a couple of items here in the museum. The first is a Newcastle United season ticket for 1899/1900. It's a white piece of paper pasted onto a blue backing-board wallet. The ticket allows access to the ground and reserved areas, and 'admits to all matches except cup ties and special matches'. It cost 15 shillings – worth about £50 today. This season ticket, number 864, belonged to William Elliott, of 40 Ash Street, Newcastle. Ash Street was in Benwell, to the west of the city centre, and directories from the time show William worked as a confectioner. His name and address are handwritten on the card, above Watt's signature. A grid of match numbers shows crosses through the matches William attended, marked off with a pen by the gateman as he entered St James' Park way back in the last days of the Victorian era.

Next to the season ticket is a share certificate from the 1896 share issue that effectively saved the club. A Mr Robinson Hudson bought five shares in the Newcastle United Football Company Ltd at 10 shillings each. They were share numbers 86 to 90. Again the certificate, creased and worn through time, is signed by the omnipresent Watt. Also on display here is a club minute book from the 1890s, open at the page that records the decision to change the club's colours to black and white. These small items might not be the most eye-catching in the exhibition, but they are surely the most important.

After perusing the Newcastle United exhibition, a wander into the Newcastle Story seems appropriate. It's a fascinating tale, of Romans, Saxons and Normans, of bridges, castles and battles. But one exhibit in particular catches the eye. It's a display board featuring the lyrics to a song sung by the people of Newcastle around the time of the Civil War in the 17th century. Remarkably, it's an anti-Sunderland song, and it goes right to the heart of explaining football's intense Tyne-Wear rivalry.

Observers from afar might not appreciate how fierce the rivalry between Newcastle and Sunderland is, but the Tyne-Wear derby is as competitive a football match as you could ever hope to see. Geordies and Mackems may be separated by a few miles and an accent, but they share a consuming passion for football. The Tyne-Wear derby is a fight for the claim to be top dog in this 'Hotbed of Soccer'. It may be seen by outsiders as a parochial battle, but within the region its importance can't be overstated. With both Newcastle and Sunderland starved of success for so much of their history, the derby match has effectively become our cup final. What you need to know about the Tyne-Wear derby is that it *really* matters.

The song lyrics displayed here in the museum illustrate that the rivalry between Newcastle and Sunderland goes back way beyond football. The song dates the rivalry back to the 17th century, but conflict between the two towns has probably been around for much longer than that. Newcastle had been battling for a monopoly over the export of coal since the time of King John in the early 1200s. By 1600, 20-times more coal was being shipped from the Tyne than from Wear. Newcastle was eventually awarded a royal charter for exclusive coal export rights, which took more trade away from Sunderland, and caused the Wearside town serious economic difficulties.

When the Civil War broke out in 1642, Newcastle understandably remained loyal to the King, Charles I, while Sunderland sided with the Parliamentarians. In effect, both towns were fighting for their livelihoods. That fight was most graphically realised at the Battle of Boldon Hill in March 1644. Having unsuccessfully attacked Newcastle, an army of Scottish Covenanters sought refuge in Sunderland. The Duke of Newcastle, the afore-mentioned William Cavendish, led his army out in pursuit, and met the Scottish army – bolstered by Wearside men – at what is now the site of the village of East Boldon.

Like many Tyne-Wear derby matches, the battle was a scrappy affair. Both sides exchanged cannon fire and engaged in hesitant skirmishes, but bad weather prevented an all-out attack. Many soldiers were killed, and both sides claimed victory, but in truth it probably ended as a draw. Sunderland continued to support the Scots, and acted as a supply base during the ongoing Siege of Newcastle. The people of Sunderland adopted the blue bonnets of the Scottish army. After holding out for more than seven months, Newcastle eventually fell to the Scots, and, as the war ended, the Parliamentarians were victorious. Charles I was executed, and Newcastle's coal monopoly was over.

It seems unsurprising, therefore, that around the time of the Civil War the people of Newcastle would sing an anti-Sunderland song: *'Ride through Sandgate, up and doon / There you'll see the gallants fighting for the croon / And all the cull cuckolds in Sunderland toon / With their bonny blew caps cannot pull them doon.'* More modern anti-Sunderland songs are mostly about football, but are no less creative.

We've previously covered the origin of the term 'Geordie', and we should probably do the same for 'Mackem'. It's derived from the Wearside pronunciation of the phrase 'make them', and probably originated in 19th century shipbuilding, where it was said that Sunderland would make the ships, and Newcastle would take them and fit them out – 'mak'em and tak'em'. Like 'Geordie', 'Mackem' may have originated as a term of abuse, in this case aimed by Newcastle shipbuilders at their Sunderland rivals. It seems to have taken much longer to have been adopted by the people of Sunderland, with the first reference in print only occurring in the late 20th century. Today, just as Newcastle United fans are known as 'Geordies', Sunderland fans are known as 'Mackems'.

Sunderland AFC began life as Sunderland and District Teachers AFC, and played their first match in November 1880, a few months before the first match of Newcastle's Stanley FC. Sunderland's first ground was actually in Hendon, at the Blue House Field. Unlike Newcastle's first ground, Sunderland's has a blue plaque mounted on a brick gatepost: 'The first home ground of what is now Sunderland AFC.'

The first competitive Newcastle-Sunderland football match didn't involve Newcastle United. It was played at St James' Park, on 12 February 1881, when Newcastle Rangers beat Sunderland 5-0 in the Northumberland and Durham Cup semi-final. (Rangers went on to win the cup in its inaugural season.) Sunderland were beaten again at St James' Park in December 1881, this time by a Newcastle FA side (who probably played in black and white stripes), and then over in Jesmond in January 1882 by Tyne Association. Further meetings between these teams followed over the next few months, and Sunderland lost all of them. Most notably, Tyne Association beat Sunderland 2-0 in the Northumberland and Durham Cup final in 1883.

We've already covered the first proper Tyne-Wear derby, played on 3 November 1883 at Heaton Junction, back when Newcastle United was still called East End. It was a friendly match, and the score was 0-0 at half-time, but the visitors eventually won 3-0, meaning that first spoils went to Sunderland. The first competitive derby was an FA Cup tie on Wearside on 17 November 1888, which Sunderland also won, this time 2-0.

That defeat for East End might not have hurt as much as it would today. At the time, the teams weren't the great footballing rivals they are now. There were scores of local teams playing at a similar level at the time, and plenty of rivalries as a result. East End had much more immediate local rivals in West End, and Sunderland had Sunderland Albion. But both West End and Sunderland Albion folded in 1892. Now the Tyne-Wear derby could begin to move towards centre stage.

Sunderland, initially, remained 'North East top dogs', under the leadership of Tom Watson. They were elected to the Football League, and soon established themselves as the best side in England, winning the Football League three times – in 1891/92, 1892/93 and 1894/95. Throughout this time, the only Tyne-Wear derby matches were occasional friendlies. Then, in 1898, Newcastle reached the first division alongside Sunderland.

The first league clash between the two teams took place in front of 30,000 fans at the Wearsiders' new Roker Park ground on Christmas Eve 1898. Tens of thousands of Geordies attempted to travel to Wearside for the game. 'Long before noon there was a lengthy queue at the special box provided outside Central Station by the North-Eastern Railway Company for the issue of tickets to Sunderland,' reported the *Journal*, 'and until half-past one o'clock there was a constant stream of people clamouring for speedy conveyance to the Wearside borough, but the company utterly failed to cope with the traffic.'

Those Newcastle folk who did make it to Roker faced more disappointment. Sunderland had raised the admission price for the derby. 'Scores of people refused to pay the additional charges, which touched the pockets of the Tynesiders the most heavily, coming as they did on top of their railway fares,' said the *Journal*. 'The Sunderland club and supporters have never been treated in like fashion at St James' Park, and they are not likely to curry favour, but rather destroy it, by such an injudicious policy.'

Once inside the new ground, the Newcastle fans impressed *Sunderland Echo* football columnist Ixion, who made another early reference to those black and white birds. 'The loud applause which greeted the "magpies" clearly indicated the immense strength of their followers in all parts of the ground,' he wrote. And the travelling fans would have thoroughly enjoyed their day - the 'magnificent' Peddie scored yet another two goals in a 3-2 win for Newcastle. 'This game was undoubtedly a revelation as well as a pleasant surprise to the supporters of Newcastle United,' said Ixion. 'In my opinion they never before played such an effective and finished game.'

As the season progressed, Newcastle managed to win enough games to survive their first season in the top flight. Only champions Aston Villa had a bigger average attendance than the Magpies. That trend continued into the following season, during which SJP experienced its first 30,000-strong crowd, for a match against Sheffield United in October 1899. The gates were shut half an hour before kick-off, locking thousands more outside, including, according to the *Sunderland Echo*, hundreds who had come up from Sunderland to see the game. (No doubt most Sunderland fans were supporting the famous Sheffield team, but it's interesting to note that the rivalry of the time allowed Sunderland fans to travel to the Newcastle ground as 'neutral' spectators.) 'The excitement was intense,' the paper reported. Unfortunately, there were no goals for the massive crowd to enjoy, but 0-0 was an impressive result for Newcastle against one of the country's best teams.

In the Newcastle side for that Sheffield United match was Joe Rogers, a quick and strapping wide man signed by Frank Watt from Grimsby Town. In November

1899 Rogers became Newcastle United's first international player – unofficially, at least. Rogers was selected for the English FA's tour of Germany and Austria. He made his debut in an incredible 10-2 victory over Germany in Berlin – and scored five goals. Despite that extraordinary effort, and the fact that he scored another two goals in subsequent games, he never played for the full England side. As the English FA XI isn't regarded as a full England 'A' team, Rogers' achievement isn't recorded in the official England record books. So Newcastle would have to wait until 1901 for their first official international player, when Matt Kingsley kept goal for the 'proper' England team.

Another key player at this time was right-half Alec Gardner, signed on another Scottish raid from Leith Athletic. An excellent midfield passer, Gardner became a pivotal member of the Magpies' Edwardian side. 'He was one of the best players in the game, with a deserved reputation as a "gentlemanly footballer",' wrote Arthur Appleton. Although Gardner would play at the top level with Newcastle for a decade, he never played for Scotland. 'It remains a mystery why he was never capped,' wrote Appleton. (Although Appleton wasn't born until 1915, and therefore never saw the likes of Gardner play – in any case, he was a Sunderland fan! – he did speak to 'old supporters' for first-hand accounts, so we can probably trust his judgement within the pages of *Hotbed of Soccer*.)

Meanwhile, as Newcastle began to secure their foothold in the first division, the Tyne-Wear rivalry grew. 'There has always been a strong rivalry between the premier clubs of Newcastle and Sunderland,' explained the *Sunderland Echo*, 'and this feeling has been greatly intensified since both clubs are making such resolute efforts to take leading honours in the league.'

On Good Friday 1901, up to 70,000 fans descended on St James' Park for a derby match. 'There was an unprecedented scene, one which perhaps never had its counterpart in any other football centre in the country,' said the *Echo*. The gates were closed 45 minutes before kick-off, with 32,000 fans packed right up to the touch-lines inside the 30,000-capacity ground. The ground was literally bursting at the seams, with up to 40,000 more fans outside trying to get in. Eventually the gates were forced open, trees were climbed, and walls were scaled. 'They clambered over the rails like cats, and then not only smashed the gates down, but also carried with them a portion of the adjoining railing,' said the *Echo*. 'Through this gap they trooped, pushing the people before them onto the playing pitch.' There were only 25 policemen on duty, and they were quickly overwhelmed: 'All opposition to their entrance by the small force of police available on the ground was set at nought.'

The situation soon became very dangerous, as the *Echo*'s remarkable account explains: 'The roofs of the reserved stands were black with people, and part of the roof gave way, causing the frightened people underneath to make a hurried departure. There was chaos everywhere, and it was readily seen that it would be impossible to clear the pitch.'

Once they realised they wouldn't be seeing a match, 'a numerous section of the rough element commenced to riot and wreck the wooden stands.' 'Heated arguments over the merits of Newcastle United and Sunderland led to numerous free fights. These comparatively common incidents developed into affairs of a more serious description. Three or four thousand persons, mostly young fellows with caps on, formed themselves into one compact body, and went on an expedition of wreckage.'

These thousands of early hooligans tore down the SJP goal-posts, despite the best attempts of a single brave policeman, who had his helmet knocked off by a falling crossbar. They climbed onto the roof of the stand, tore down the club's black and white flag, and ripped it to shreds. The tiny band of police drew their batons and charged the huge mob, and somehow held them at bay until reinforcements arrived on horseback. Many people were hurt in the melee, in the crush to escape, or in falls from the roof of the stand. Incredibly, although several people were taken to the infirmary, no one was killed.

After the dust had settled, thoughts turned to the £970 that had been taken at the turnstiles. The Sunderland press demanded that the away fans should be reimbursed, but United, quite reasonably, said it couldn't return the money because it was impossible to say who had paid and who had not. Instead, the money was used to repair the damage. One Sunderland fan did sue Newcastle for his entrance money, but he lost the case and was ordered to pay £70 in costs. The match was replayed a few weeks later, and there was more calamity for Newcastle as Sunderland won 2-0.

Sunderland finished as runners up in the first division that season, behind Tom Watson's Liverpool, and then won the league title in 1901/02. But that was the end of the line for the 'Team of All Talents'. The North East top dogs title was about to be passed on. Sunderland's greatest period was ending, and Newcastle's was about to begin.

So we're leaving the Discovery Museum and the Victorian era behind. Queen Victoria died in January 1901, and was succeeded by her son, Edward VI. So began the short but significant Edwardian era. It was the era of the electric tram and the motor car, David Lloyd George and Joseph Chamberlain, the Wright brothers and Dr Crippen, Edward Elgar and George Bernard Shaw, Captain Scott and Ernest Shackleton, Bisto and Meccano. Most significantly, it was the era of Newcastle United.

Newcastle United Ogden's cigarette card

Newcastle players emerge from the Gallowgate end tunnel at St James' Park ahead of the Liverpool match, 23 November 1901
Left to right: Alex Caie, Bob McColl, Bob Bennie, Jock Peddie
Also pictured, behind Bennie, are Tom Watson and Frank Watt

Opposite page:
Newcastle fans at St James' Park, and a rare glimpse of the Victorian West Stand (photos courtesy BFI National Archive)

8

The Combination Game

It's Saturday 23 November 1901, and a wintry mist hangs over Newcastle. You finish work at midday, hands grubby and aching, and hurry home to scrub up. In the tin bath on the kitchen floor, you read the newspaper, its pages focussing on Lord Kitchener's command of the Boer War. But it's the football column that's of most interest. 'The McColl Sensation!' reads the headline, above a story about Newcastle's latest big money signing. Then there are today's fixtures, including, at St James' Park, Newcastle versus reigning Football League champions Liverpool.

You put on your shirt and tie, suit and flat cap, and hurry out to meet your mates, riding on a brake into the city centre, along roads that are yet to be introduced to electric trams. A couple of pints in the packed, smoky inns on Barrack Road, and then it's into St James' Park, handing over sixpence to the gateman, and manoeuvring into position on the banked terrace. You're one of 20,000 fans packed inside, swaying and cheering ahead of the match.

There are open terraces at three sides of the ground, with bobbing heads visible all the way to the back, and a row of fans standing perched along the top edges. Leazes Terrace and the townhouses of St James' Street are visible behind the east terrace. Smoke billows from chimney stacks, and net curtains can be seen in the windows. At the west side of the ground is the timber stand with its covered roof. On top of the roof is a small elevated press box. Around the pitch are advertising hoardings, for Oxo, Murton's department store ('for all kinds of sports and pastimes'), and most prominently for Newton's of Westgate Road, a retailer of 'perambulators' – or babies' prams.

It's possible to give a pretty specific description of the scene inside St James's Park on this particular day. Up until this point, everything we know about Newcastle United has been drawn from newspapers and minute books, photographs and sketches, and other valuable paper documents from which the club's history can be extrapolated. But on that misty day in November 1901, for the very first time, a Newcastle United match was captured on film.

The silent, flickering footage is grey and scratchy, but remarkably clear given its age. It places the viewer inside the Edwardian St James' Park, surrounded by a living, breathing mass of fans. The players, previously just names in match reports and faces in team photos, suddenly come alive.

The film was shot by Mitchell and Kenyon, the topical filmmakers who documented early 20th century Britain using hand-cranked cameras. It was found, alongside hundreds of other Mitchell and Kenyon films, inside a metal drum in the basement of an old Blackburn toy shop in 1994. It's since been restored and preserved by the British Film Institute. It's a remarkable piece of history, one of the earliest football films in existence. It's the nearest we can get without a time machine to experiencing the early days of Newcastle United.

The seven-minute film captures one of the biggest matches of the season, but the focus isn't particularly on the match action. Almost half of the film is devoted to the crowd. It was difficult to film the action – Mitchell and Kenyon's fixed and heavy cameras couldn't be moved quickly enough to pan across the pitch, and also film was too expensive to roll for a full 90 minutes. But, most importantly, Mitchell and Kenyon wanted to get as many fans as possible on camera in the knowledge that people would pay to see themselves and their friends on screen. Moving pictures were new and exciting. There was no cinema or newsreel at this time, and seeing yourself onscreen must have felt like a magical experience.

The film was commissioned by Arthur Duncan Thomas, an eccentric showman who operated under the banner Edison-Thomas Pictures in a brazen attempt to confuse people into thinking he might be the great Thomas Edison. After being shot at St James' Park in the afternoon, the film was screened at a Newcastle theatre in the evening. So rather than going home to watch *Match of the Day* like their modern equivalents, Edwardian fans could have crowded into the city's Palace or Empire Theatre and watched, no doubt in awe, as the moving pictures panned across their faces.

Both the Palace and Empire, which were on Percy Street and Newgate Street, have been demolished. But to get an idea of what it must have been like to have watched this first Newcastle United footage I'm heading along Westgate Road to the Tyne Theatre, which was opened by Joseph Cowen in 1867, and back in 1901 was called the Tyne Theatre and Opera House.

The theatre and several surrounding buildings look pretty much as they would have done back in the Edwardian era. Heading up from the Discovery Museum, we can turn into Westgate Road past a big brick building with a mural on the exposed gable end that reads 'The Robert Sinclair Tobacco Coy Ltd'. Sinclair had been selling tobacco on Westgate Road since the 1890s, and in 1898 his company produced the first full set of Newcastle United cigarette cards. One of Newcastle's most successful businessmen, Sinclair later became the chairman of Imperial Tobacco.

There were at least eight pubs along this stretch of Westgate Road in 1901, including the Black Bull, which is now the location of the Bodega. There were also jewellers, newsagents, confectioners and cabinet makers. Just past the Tyne Theatre was a police and fire station. The Tyne Theatre was actually turned into a cinema in 1919, being temporarily renamed the Stoll Picture House. There's a sign above the door of the Grade I listed building that still bears this name, and there's a mural on the side of the building that says 'The Stoll: Tyneside's Talkie Theatre'. Back in 1901, though, there were no cinemas, no 'talkies', and very few films.

The Tyne Theatre is relatively small compared to the Palace and Empire, seating around 1,100 audience members, compared to 2,000 or 3,000. But inside the ornate horseshoe-shaped auditorium, with three tiered balconies stacked over the stalls, it's easy to get a sense of the excitement that must have surrounded this remarkable screening. Most of those present would never have seen moving pictures before, and would certainly never have seen themselves on screen. It's difficult to appreciate in the modern era of camera phones and 'selfies', but in 1901 many of those present would never have even seen themselves in a still photograph.

If you've ever seen footage of the famous Lumière brothers film *Train Pulling Into Station*, where the audience leaps from their seats in the belief that the train onscreen is actually pulling into the theatre, then you'll have a good idea of the impact early films could have on audiences at this time. Add to the mix the fact that this audience could have enjoyed a few hours of post-match drinking before the screening, and you can get a sense of the noisy, uproarious, excited atmosphere that must have prevailed. As the curtains opened, revealing Mitchell and Kenyon's screen onstage, the sense of expectation must have been utterly thrilling.

The film opens with shots of the expectant St James' crowd, taking their seats in the pavilion, and packing into the terraces. They wear flat caps and bowler hats, and most are in smart suits with pocket squares. Some of the younger men wear stiff-necked shirts with upright collars – an uncomfortable fashion at the time. They jostle for space, waving hats, handkerchiefs and newspapers at the camera, keen to be recorded for history. There's at least one lady visible in the pavilion, and several children dotted around the ground. Some fans offer regal waves, then laugh with their mates as the camera passes. It's clear they are having a royal good time. There are plenty of moustaches on show, and many fans are smoking, sending puffs of white smoke into the air above their heads. One fan lifts a small child above his head, and an amused bobby, his policeman's helmet fixed with a chin strap, smiles at the camera.

Obviously, it's a silent film, but there would have been plenty of noise in the ground. We know that the club's fans had previously chanted 'Play up East End!', and that may well have been updated to 'Play up Newcastle!' Early football chants were often rude and lewd. The Victorian author Charles Edwards wrote that early football fans used 'a number of emphatic and even mysterious expletives', with 'workaday adjectives very loose on their tongues.' 'Supporters often forget themselves in the ferocity of their cries,' said Edwards. '"Down him!" "Sit on his chest!" "Knock their ribs in!"'

But many early football exhortations were more positive, as fans displayed their enthusiasm. 'How keenly the onlookers watch the game! How well they appreciate and note every little display of science!' wrote a correspondent for *Chums* magazine. 'A running fire of cheers accompanies a favourite player as he sprints and dodges down the line. The cries grow deeper as he nears the goal, and culminate in a very roar as he kicks the ball through it.'

We know that fans sang at matches from at least the 1880s, particularly during the wait before kick-off. They joined together for communal singing of patriotic ditties like *Rule Britannia*, and music hall numbers like *Two Lovely*

Black Eyes. There were few more popular music hall numbers on Tyneside than *Blaydon Races*, which shares a Victorian heritage with Newcastle United. Written by famous local troubadour Geordie Ridley in 1862, the song was sung by performers in concert halls and by kids playing in the streets, with its lyrics distributed in popular song books (alongside other Geordie Ridley favourites that aren't as well-remembered today, such as *Joey Jones*, *Johnny Luik-Up* and *The Bobby Cure*). Ridley himself had died in 1864, aged just 30, long before football arrived in Newcastle. But it's entirely possible that Newcastle United's early fans sang his *Blaydon Races* with just as much lustre as their modern equivalents do today.

As the film rolls on, the first team out onto the pitch is Liverpool, in red shirts and white knickerbockers, with belts holding up their shorts, led from the players' tunnel by Scottish international Alex Raisbeck. The tunnel is behind the goal at the Gallowgate end, rather than its present position in the middle of the west end of the ground. The visitors are followed out by the referee, Mr Bye, in a thick moustache and suit and tie, with a cap on his head and a pocket watch hanging from a chain. It's clearly a chilly day, and puffs of warm breath are visible from the players' mouths.

There's then a lovely moment captured at the tunnel entrance. Liverpool secretary/manager Tom Watson and Newcastle secretary/manager Frank Watt, both cheerful-looking moustachioed chaps in bowler hats and trench coats, wander out to the end of the entrance tunnel, jovially chatting and smiling. Watson is the more portly of the two. With the addition of a false beard, he would have made a fine toy shop Santa Claus. Fans who must recognise Watson from his time at Newcastle lean over the tunnel to say hello and shake his hand. Watson sucks on a cigar, and Watt also lights up a smoke, both grinning through their 'taches. This really was a meeting of great minds. Watson had built Newcastle's foundations, and Watt was building its future. It would have been fascinating to overhear their conversation, a priceless meeting between two of the most important characters in the club's history.

As the film continues, Newcastle are led out by their cleanly-shaven and neatly-coiffured captain Andy Aitken, who bounces a laced leather caser in front of him. As he passes, he shares a joke with Tom Watson, then dropkicks the ball out onto the pitch. Aitken was now well-established as Newcastle's captain and leader, as influential on the pitch as Watt was off it. He usually played at half-back, but was incredibly versatile. He'd recently made his international debut for Scotland. 'Plays equally well in any position – back, half-back, or forward, and vows he will finish in goal,' read a pen portrait in the *Glasgow Evening Telegraph*. 'An indefatigable worker; excels in covering up backs and assisting forwards.' Aitken was nicknamed 'the Daddler', which most likely referred to a perceived 'dawdling' playing style, although 'daddle' also meant 'fist', so it may have referred to his aptitude as a pugilist.

Following Aitken, strapping left-half Jack Carr takes a last drag on a smoke – a wonderful period touch. Carr, from Seaton Burn, was (to borrow that much-used cliché) a fantastic servant to the club throughout the Edwardian era, and arguably one of the most valuable yet least cele-brated players in Newcastle United's history. Despite his penchant for smoking, he made almost 300 appearances for the club, and also played a couple of times for Eng-land. He was a Magpie for almost 25 years as a player and a coach.

The Newcastle players, all broad-shouldered and barrel-chested, wear long-sleeved black and white shirts tucked into knee-length knickerbockers, with dark socks and leather ankle boots. A young lad who seems to work for the club taps them on the back as they enter the field. The lad may be Frank Watt Junior, who would grow up to become assistant secretary of the club – and would take over as secretary after the death of his father.

Most of the players ignore the camera, except for right-back Bob Bennie, who pauses and grins into the lens. Goalkeeper Matt Kingsley, moustachioed and wear-ing a cap, wears a noticeably different black and white shirt with a black hooped neck rather than a button-up like his team-mates – probably to prevent his loose collar from being grabbed by opposition forwards. Although he isn't wearing gloves when he enters the field, he is by the time the action gets underway – big black things that look more like mittens than modern goalie gloves.

Big Jock Peddie, six feet tall and almost as wide, looks pretty intimidating, and it's obvious why defenders feared him. With a long, pallid face, he has something of Lurch from *The Addams Family* about him. Also visible is Ron Orr, another long-serving player, a Scottish interna-tional, who would later end up moving from Newcastle to Liverpool. A few weeks earlier, Newcastle had thrashed

Notts County 8-0, with Peddie scoring a hat-trick and Orr scoring four. Next out of the tunnel is another forward, Alex Caie, a new signing from Milwall Athletic who played 35 times for Newcastle but only scored a single goal.

And then, last but certainly not least, comes Newcastle's latest signing, a Scotsman called Robert Smyth 'Bob' McColl. If the name sounds familiar from a non-football setting, that's because RS McColl founded what would become the country's largest chain of newsagents in 1901, shortly before moving to Newcastle. But back then he was much better known as a footballer – one of the best Scotland had ever produced. He'd go on to play an important part in this game – and in the history of Newcastle United.

A forward formerly with the influential Queen's Park club, McColl was an established Scotland international and a prolific scorer. In 1899/1900, in a remarkable feat of net-busting, he'd scored a hat-trick of international hat-tricks, against Wales, Northern Ireland and England. Frank Watt would certainly have known all about McColl, and might have been tempted to poach the player on one his many excursions north of the border. However, he didn't need to. McColl actually turned up in Newcastle and offered to sign for the club – if the price was right.

The 'McColl Sensation' trumpeted about in newspapers was the huge revelation that Newcastle had paid the player a £50 signing on fee, with 'remarkable wages' of £6 10s a week – a record at the time. Queen's Park was a famously amateur club, and McColl had been an amateur player. So this was quite an introduction to the professional game. But money may not have been the only reason McColl choose Newcastle. Geography probably played a part, too – it wasn't too far from his Glasgow home, and the move offered him the opportunity to expand his newsagent business into England. The presence of Scottish international teammate Andy Aitken would also have helped. Aitken was a tactical thinker, and in McColl he would have seen a like-minded character who could bring valuable know-how to Newcastle.

Despite their amateur status, McColl's former club Queen's Park had a strong reputation, and were credited with introducing to football the 'combination' game – which basically involved short passing and teamwork. This 'scientific' approach had spread throughout Scotland, and had allowed the national team to gain dominance over England, where kick and run was still the order of the day. McColl, known as 'the prince of centre-forwards', was an intelligent exponent of the combination game. At Newcastle, he set about teaching his teammates the tricks of his trade. In doing so he set them up to become the most progressive and forward-thinking team of the Edwardian era.

In the film, McColl looks remarkably slight as he casts a pensive look at the camera. It's clear why he would have preferred a skilful passing game to a more physical kick and run. The Liverpool match was his second game for the club. He'd made his debut against Manchester City in the previous week – and scored from the penalty spot in a 3-0 win.

The match action caught on film is frenetic. There

are few signs of Bob McColl's yet-to-be-passed-on passing game and much more prevalent are wild kicks and clumsy challenges. Although the film is silent, we can imagine these moments must have elicited wild cheers and laughs from the theatre audience. At one point a Newcastle player clatters a Liverpool opponent, and the referee peeps on his whistle. The Liverpool player is helped up, with a teammate rubbing his injured knee, and the game continues.

We also get to see the early version of the penalty area, which in 1901 wasn't a box but instead consisted of two arcs drawn using a rope tied to the goal-posts, producing a shape that unavoidably resembles a cartoonish pair of breasts.

Newcastle seem to have the best of the play, as the ball flashes across the visitors' penalty area, and is punched away by the Liverpool keeper. Big Jock Peddie is involved in a couple of goalmouth scrambles, but can't quite put the ball in the net. The main sense you get from this footage is of how extremely fast and physical the early Edwardian game was. Forget the Mr Cholmondly-Warner image of gentlemanly 'after you, sir' tippy-tappy football. This was tough and demanding stuff. There's a widespread perception that players from the past couldn't hold a candle to the stars of today. But there's no doubt from this film that you had to be pretty good to play first division football in 1901.

Unfortunately, Mitchell and Kenyon's clunky camera missed the winning goal, a 25-yard dipping shot from Bob McColl that flew over the goalkeeper's head and under the bar. We have to rely on newspaper reports to learn about that. Reports also tell us that at one point a ball was booted onto the roof of the stand and couldn't be retrieved. And, towards the end of the match, Liverpool's Charlie Satterthwaite crashed head-first into one of the advertising hoardings and had to be carried unconscious from the pitch.

After watching the footage looped several times, the audience would have spilled out of the theatre onto the streets of Newcastle, past newsboys selling the recently-launched *Football Pink*, and into the pubs to discuss the film and the match. It's at this point that it's easy to identify with these early Edwardian supporters, as they pack into the city's many pubs, jostle for the bar, and raise a glass to their football team. It's a scene that will be familiar to any fan of the modern era.

Mitchell and Kenyon never returned to St James' Park, although they did film Newcastle at Goodison Park in September 1902. Again the cameras missed the only goal of the game, but they did capture Newcastle's scorer Willie Stewart walking back to the halfway line and receiving a cordial handshake and pat on the back.

Leaving the Tyne Theatre and continuing down Westgate Road, we come to Central Station. It was designed by the great North Shields-born architect John Dobson, and built in the 1840s by Robert Stephenson, the son of Geordie railway pioneer George Stephenson. Robert also built the magnificent wrought iron-arched High Level Bridge, which allowed the London to Edinburgh railway line to cross the Tyne. The rail link between Newcastle and London would prove useful in subsequent seasons, and the Newcastle United story will pass back through Central Station soon.

Newcastle finished the 1901/02 season in third place, an excellent achievement for this emerging team. Sunderland were league champions, but it would be Wearside's last taste of silverware for some time. The two sides clashed in the FA Cup that season at St James' Park. The game had already been postponed due to a snow-storm, and there were rumours that it could be abandoned again due to snow on the pitch. However, perhaps fearful of what had happened in the previous year, the match went ahead, bad weather and all. Newcastle won 1-0 courtesy of a goal from Ron Orr.

In the following season, Newcastle dealt Sunderland a much more painful bloody nose in a match that decided the league championship. It was the last game of the season, on 25 April 1903, and high-flying Sunderland needed a victory at St James' Park to leapfrog The Wednesday and retain the league title. Newspapers in Sheffield underestimated the Tyne-Wear rivalry, and expected Newcastle to roll over in favour of Sunderland. 'To United the match means nothing, but to Sunderland everything,' said the *Sheffield Evening Telegraph*, 'and owing to the fact that the clubs are such near neighbours, it has been stated in some quarters that there is a possibility that the Newcastle club will not exert every effort to win.'

Newcastle swiftly put out a statement saying that all of its players would be 'doing their level best'. 'Well I do not suppose that anyone imagined that they would say anything else,' responded the *Evening Telegraph*. But the newspaper's cynicism was misplaced.

More than 26,000 fans saw Newcastle produce an effective display of combination football, an approach now successfully implemented by Bob McColl. 'The football was keen, lively and bracing,' said one reporter. And, just before half-time, McColl served up a brilliant example of his short passing style, starting a move, combining with Alec Gardner, then finishing from close range. Newcastle won the match 1-0, and The Wednesday won the league championship, with Sunderland heading home empty-handed. A Newcastle newspaper headline read: 'Doubting Thomases Demoralised!'

Newcastle struck Sunderland with another blow in the following season, 1903/04, when they signed Sunderland's best player Andy McCombie for a Football League record fee of £700. The Scottish international was described as 'a dour, dogged tackler, hard to beat as he possesses rare speed and lots of weight, and is not afraid to use either'. But he was skilful too. The *Chronicle*'s Tom Coulthard called McCombie 'Dainty Feet', explaining that he was as 'dainty on his feet as a dancer'.

A quiet chap off the field, McCombie was a piano tuner by trade. ('As a relief to the hurly-burly of the football field, McCombie finds pianoforte-tuning a recuperative and not unrenumerative employment for his leisure hours,' remarks his profile in early football book *Association Football and the Men Who Made It*.) But he'd had a big falling out with Sunderland over the sum of £100 received from the chairman of the club. McCombie believed the sum was a gift, and was somewhat aggrieved when he was later asked to repay it. He was dropped from the squad, and approached by virtually every top first division club. Luckily, he chose Newcastle.

And McCombie wasn't the only newcomer to the Newcastle team. There was Jack Rutherford, 'the Newcastle Flyer', a quick-as-a-blink local winger who scored on his debut aged just 17, and would soon play for England. According to Arthur Appleton, 'he had a dart-like speed, neat ball control, and the ability to cut in and score'. Appleton regarded Rutherford as one of 'the best of Newcastle's local discoveries', and said that Frank Watt regarded him as Newcastle's greatest outside-right. Jack was also the great-grandfather of Olympic long jump champion Greg Rutherford.

Peter McWilliam, a young Scottish left-half, was poached by Newcastle from under the nose of Sunderland. McWilliam was travelling by train to meet with Sunderland officials, but stopped off at Newcastle to see his sister, who ran a café in the city. Frank Watt heard of his visit, intercepted him at the station, and signed him on the platform. Tom Coulthard said McWilliam was 'popularly believed to be possessed of India-rubber legs, and developed a famous little body wriggle that was annoyingly deceptive.'

Then there was Jimmy Howie, 'Gentleman James', another Scot, and a goal-scoring inside right, signed from Bristol Rovers for a big £300 fee. *Association Football and the Men Who Made It* devotes a section to Howie, and mentions his 'peculiar running action', which made it appear that he was hopping, but afforded him extraordinarily close control of the ball. 'The manner in which he worms his way through the serried ranks of the opposition with the ball at his toes, changing legs at every stride, and feinting for an opening either to kick or pass, is amazing to the onlooker,' says the *Association Football* book. 'Despite his scratchy action, he can move to some tune.'

Bill Appleyard was a big and burly centre-forward, signed from Grimsby Town to replace Jock Peddie. 14-stone Appleyard became hugely popular with fans for his barnstorming displays and stacks of goals. His nickname was Cockles, because he'd worked as a cockle fisherman before becoming a footballer. The similarly-surnamed Arthur Appleton wrote that Appleyard 'brought sheer punch to the centre, and there was sufficient skill about him for the ball to be put on his right – his good – side.' Tom Coulthard wrote, 'When Bill swung his foot at the ball it was invariably a "net smasher".' Unfortunately, Appleyard was injury prone, and that factor restricted his appearances for Newcastle. Nevertheless, he managed to score 87 goals in 145 games, giving him a better goals-to-games ratio than either Shearer or Milburn.

And then there was one other player who became a regular during the 1903/04 season. He was a local lad, from Heaton, who'd actually made his debut back in October 1899, aged 18. Incredibly versatile, he made various appearances across the outfield, before establishing himself at half-back. His name was Colin Veitch, and he would go on to become arguably the greatest player in the history of Newcastle United. There'll be a lot more about him very soon.

Propelled by the goals of Howie and Appleyard, Newcastle finished fourth in the league in 1903/04. For a time they were genuine title contenders, offering a tantalising preview of what was to come. At the end of the season, Bob McColl returned to Scotland, and signed for Glasgow Rangers. He'd been at Newcastle for less than three seasons, but he'd had a huge impact. His combination game was adopted and adapted by Andy Aitken and his teammates, and would serve the club very well over the next few years. The Magpies were about to enter the most successful period in the club's history.

*'Lord Beresford kicking off' a Newcastle vs Sunderland friendly
match to mark the visit of the Channel Fleet to the River Tyne,
St James' Park, 27 September 1904*

*Peter McWilliam, Jimmy Howie and Bill Appleyard,
from The Book of Football, 1905*

Newcastle's 1905 FA Cup Final team at the Crystal Palace
Newcastle lost their first cup final 2-0 to Aston Villa
Pictured left to right: Jimmy McPherson (trainer), Peter
McWilliam, Jack Rutherford, Jimmy Howie, Alec Gardner, Andy
Aitken, Colin Veitch, Jimmy Lawrence, Bill Appleyard, Andy
McCombie, Jack Carr, Bert Gosnell, Frank Watt (secretary)

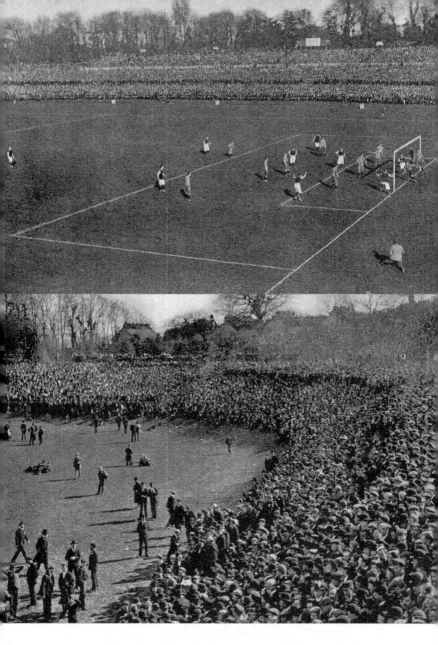

Scenes from the Crystal Palace, Newcastle vs Aston Villa,
FA Cup Final, 15 April 1905

9

The League

If you want to see what Newcastle upon Tyne looked like during Newcastle United's formative years, then the trick is to look up. Above the shop windows and pub doorways, Newcastle is a remarkably well-preserved city, its streets lined with grand Georgian and Victorian buildings, particularly around the Grainger Town area. It's said of the great builder Richard Grainger that he 'found Newcastle of bricks and timber and left it in stone'. He was born right at the heart of what is now named Grainger Town. Along with architect John Dobson and town clerk John Clayton, he built much of the city that we know today. Grainger died in 1861, so he wasn't around to witness the birth and growth of Newcastle United. But the club was born into a city that he had made great.

My journey around the city continues along Grainger Street, from Central Station up to Grey's Monument. It's a street that's lined with impressive sandstone buildings with pillared frontage and vertical dormers. Halfway along Grainger Street is the Bigg Market, named not for its size, but because it was the venue of a weekly grain market, with 'bigg' being a type of barley. Bigg was used to make beer, and the Bigg Market remains associated with booze, being famous for its array of lively pubs. Now as was then, because back in 1904 the Bigg Market and adjacent Groat Market and Cloth Market were also full of pubs, including the Half Moon Inn, which still exists (under a different name - Popworld) today.

In the summer of 1904 Newcastle United left their home city to embark on their first ever European tour, journeying by steamboat to Denmark, where they beat Copenhagen club KB (Kobenhavns Boldklub) 6-1 in an impressive first victory on foreign soil. They also beat a Copenhagen XI and a Denmark XI, plus a travelling Southampton side, before returning to England – where more European opposition awaited.

Among the Newcastle party that travelled to Denmark was a young Irish defender named Bill McCracken. He'd been signed by Newcastle, against much competition, from the Belfast Distillery team for £50 – although there were suspicions of other 'inducements'. It would take McCracken a while to dislodge the excellent Jack Carr from the first team, but once he did he was quick to establish himself as one of the outstanding backs in football. He'd famously leave a major imprint on the game, perfecting the offside trap to such a ruthlessly efficient extent that the offside rule had to be changed, from the 'three opponents' rule to the 'two opponents' rule, requiring only two opponents to be ahead of an attacker when he plays the ball.

McCracken was joined at United by a young Scottish goalkeeper, Jimmy Lawrence, who had played for Glasgow Perthshire and Hibernian. Tom Coulthard of the

Chronicle said Lawrence was 'brilliant in goal', but pinpointed a weakness, saying he 'was not too happy with the crosses that came high from the left'. Nevertheless, Lawrence provided strong competition for Charlie Watts, the betting-daft keeper who would have horse racing results relayed to him by fans as he stood between the sticks during games. McCracken and Lawrence would go on to be two of the longest-serving and most successful players in Newcastle's history.

But first that European opposition, a 'Paris XI', who arrived at St James' Park at the beginning of the 1904/05 season as part of a British tour. The visiting team was referred to in press reports as 'a leading French association club'. Some sources named them as FC Paris, the football arm of the Club Athletique de Paris. However, that wasn't quite correct. 'As a matter of fact they were but a scratch lot collected by an enterprising man of business,' revealed one newspaper.

The dubious nature of the visiting team was laid bare by the scoreline. Newcastle won 11-2, with big Bill Appleyard scoring five goals. Only around 3,500 turned up to watch the match at a time when the average attendance at St James' Park was well over 20,000, indicating that the Tyneside public weren't fooled by the French team's fake credentials. As their tour continued, the Paris XI also played Woolwich Arsenal, who won 26-1. Bob Watson scored seven, and it remains Arsenal's biggest-ever victory.

Newcastle also played a friendly against Sunderland at the beginning of the 1904/05 season, to commemorate the arrival of the Channel Fleet on the Tyne. The St

James' attendance was boosted by many visiting seamen who, according to a reporter from the *Monthly Review*, 'were massed at one end of the enclosure, where the contrasting colours of the sailors and marines greatly added to the picturesqueness of the scene'.

Admiral Lord Charles Beresford was given the honour of kicking off. A wonderful photo exists, showing the Admiral standing in the centre circle, wearing a frock coat and top hat. Bunting is strung above the packed open terraces, and folk can be seen hanging out of the windows of Leazes Terrace and St James' Street, watching the spectacle unfold. 'Having survived the ordeal of being photographed in close proximity of the ball,' wrote the reporter, the Admiral, 'walked back a few paces, then with a running kick despatched the sphere well down the field, and, amid the cheers of the throng, beat a more or less rapid retreat.'

It was a big event and an exciting match. Colin Veitch started for Newcastle – he can be seen standing with his hands on his hips in the photograph. Bill Appleyard scored yet another Magpies goal. But the day ended in disappointment for Geordie fans as Newcastle lost 2-1.

My wander through the greatest city in the world has brought us me Grey's Monument, a 140ft-high tribute to Earl Charles Grey, the Alnwick-born prime minister, political reformer and tea aficionado. It's possible to go up the monument, via a spiral staircase, to a viewing platform alongside the statue of Earl Grey, which was sculpted by Edward Hodges Baily, who also crafted the statue of Lord Nelson that stands in Trafalgar Square. Behind Earl Grey is what remains of Old Eldon Square (then, of course, just plain Eldon Square). In front of him is the street that bears his name, majestically sweeping down from the city centre towards the Tyne.

There are architectural treasures along the length of Grey Street, including the Theatre Royal on the left, and the Bank of England building on the right. But it's the great curve of Grey Street that makes it really special. It is surely the greatest street in England. But don't just take my word for it. Listen to Sir John Betjeman, who said, 'As for the curve of Grey Street, I shall never forget seeing it to perfection, traffic-less on a misty Sunday morning. Not even Regent Street, even old Regent Street, London, can compare with that descending subtle curve.'

It was against the backdrop of this magnificent city that Newcastle United embarked on a remarkable season. They were now regarded as one of the best teams and biggest clubs in the county, and were among the favourites to win silverware. During 1904/05, Newcastle would overtake Aston Villa as best supported club in country, with average crowds of 21,250. They had a new-look team, missing Bob McColl, but with Andy Aitken still captain, and Frank Watt still secretary, driving the club forwards on and off the pitch.

The club's chairman at this time was John Cameron, a Scottish-born 'commercial traveller' who lived in Heaton, and had been one of the original East End shareholders back in 1890. Among the other directors were vice-chairman Joseph Bell, a colourful and popular character, and James Lunn, a local politician who lived in Old Eldon Square and would go on to succeed Cameron as chairman.

Another very important character behind the scenes was new trainer James Q McPherson. He was essentially the first team coach, and while the secretary and committee picked the team (the club didn't have a 'manager' until 1930), the trainer was responsible for improving their fitness, preparing them for matches, and treating injuries with massage and a 'magic sponge'. Like Newcastle's other senior figures John Cameron, Frank Watt and Andy Aitken, Jimmy McPherson (sometimes referred to as 'Sandy') was a Scot. He had previously been the trainer at Kilmarnock, and had rare European experience as he had worked in the emerging German football league.

The arrival of McPherson was greatly appreciated by Andy Aitken, who hadn't enjoyed the methods of previous trainer Tommy Dodds. Writing a few years later, Aitken said that Dodds had 'put us through our work in such a way as to practically make the whole team stale before the New Year dawned.' According to Aitken, Dodds' training regime began practically every morning with an eight-mile walk, followed by a bath. In the afternoon, Dodds made the players hit a punch-ball for half an hour. 'He saw to it that it was half an hour, too,' said Aitken, 'for he would stand with his watch in his hand, and you left the ball when he told you to. Naturally, we were very sore with such vigorous exercise.'

Jimmy McPherson introduced what Aitken called 'a more excellent way' of training, centred around kicking a football. 'Instead of making players sore and leg weary, why not give them the ball?' said Aitken. 'My contention is that kicking is the finest training you can have, with walking and punching the ball inbetween.' McPherson also recognised that not all players were the same, and tailored his routines to bring out the best in each individual. 'A good trainer who knows his work will study each man's constitution, and train him accordingly,' wrote Aitken.

In subsequent years, McPherson revealed another secret of maintaining his players' constitution, putting his name to newspaper adverts endorsing Andrew's Liver Salts and Oxo. ('I have great pleasure in stating that I have found Oxo invaluable to my team.')

An interesting 'behind-the-scenes' peek at the club during this period can be found in JH Morrison's chapter on Newcastle in *The Book of Football*. Club officials boasted that they had 'the best-conducted body of men in the league', Morrison says. Interestingly, he also says the club promoted a recruitment policy that refused any player who displayed 'undesirable roughness' on the field or 'unsuitable credentials' off it. The players' favourite pastime, Morrison tells us, was billiards, which they would play on the morning of a match to relax. Bill Appleyard was the club's billiards champion, and was said to be able to beat any footballer in the league at the game.

Except for fixtures at Sunderland and Middlesbrough, the team had long journeys to away matches, and clocked up, Morrison estimates, between 9,000 and 10,000 miles each season. The team travelled in a two-compartment saloon provided by the North-Eastern Railway Company. To kill time they would play solo whist, and also play pranks on the ticket inspector by switching compartments during his head count. 'They are great practical jokers,' wrote Morrison.

They were also superstitious. While driving to the ground they considered it 'a sure indication of success' if they passed a wedding party. Passing a funeral procession, on the other hand, meant certain defeat. Another firm suspicion required the team to be led onto the pitch by vice-chairman 'Uncle Joe' Bell. 'It is a very rare occasion when Uncle Joe fails to materialise,' said Morrison, 'and it is even rarer to find a victory recorded in his absence.'

After an away match, they would often have to jump straight into a hansom cab in their kit to catch the last train back to Newcastle. On one occasion, after a match at Blackburn's Ewood Park, the team's horse-drawn cab raced through the streets at such speed that the driver was brought before magistrates and fined 40 shillings.

The 1904/05 season began with a 3-0 win over Woolwich Arsenal, followed up with great home wins over title rivals Everton and Manchester City. In fact, Newcastle only lost twice at home all season. Unfortunately, one of those occasions was in the last home match of the season against Sunderland, a defeat that threatened to derail the Magpies' title challenge.

Meanwhile, there was a major distraction – the FA Cup. Newcastle had never been past the third round (which, in Edwardian times, was effectively the quarter final stage), but that changed in 1904/05. Not that the cup campaign got off to a particularly impressive start. It took them two replays to get past Plymouth Argyle in the first round, then another replay to get past Spurs in the second. A good away win at Bolton in the third round put

Newcastle into the semi-finals.

At the neutral venue of Hyde Road in Manchester – then home to Manchester City – Jimmy Howie scored the only goal of the game to beat The Wednesday. Newcastle had reached their first FA Cup final, and would travel to London and the old Crystal Palace ground to play Aston Villa.

The Crystal Palace itself was a huge plate-glass building, located in a large park at Sydenham Hill in South London. Within the park, set in a natural basin, was a large football ground, which became known as the Crystal Palace ground. From 1895 it replaced the Oval as England's national football ground.

'The great charm of the Crystal Palace was that it was so utterly unlike any other place where football was played,' wrote the journalist Jimmy Catton. 'The sports arena at the Palace was not a building. It was just a space – sylvan, verdant, luscious – God's work.' Surrounded by trees, and overlooked by an old switchback railway rollercoaster ride, it was an unusually charming and pleasant venue. But Newcastle would come to hate it.

For the first – but most definitely not the last – time, Tyneside was struck by cup fever. More than 101,000 attended the final, at least 25,000 of whom were thought to have travelled from Newcastle. Most of them would never have visited the capital before, and many would never have strayed outside of the North East. But, ahead of the match on 15 April 1905, hundreds of packed trains, boats and omnibuses headed down to London. Newspapers printed photos showing fans arriving in London on steamers and charabancs. They disembarked, wide-eyed and excited, and set about exploring the capital's sights. But they weren't universally welcomed.

Whenever northern teams reached the FA Cup final, which during the Edwardian era was every single season, London newspapers published condescending articles about the provincial invaders. The *Daily Mirror* printed a particularly astonishing example ahead of Newcastle's visit. 'The average Londoner does not pretend to understand the football excursionist from the North,' said the paper. 'On Cup-tie day he is confirmed in his opinion that industrial England is a very strange place, containing an almost alien people. He cannot understand their language. He is openly amused at their clothing. Why do they all – every one of them – wear caps? And why do they hang together in curious little groups? Possibly the Londoner cannot understand the feeling of amazement inspired in the visitors by the great city.'

Such talk failed to wipe the smiles off the faces of the travelling Newcastle fans, who were pictured grinning and smoking as they descended on the Crystal Palace, smartly dressed in their best suits, not all wearing caps – some wearing bowlers. They clutched newspapers containing illustrated match previews showing the expected team line-ups. There were no replica kits or scarves in those days, but some fans pushed black and white 'play-up' cards into their hat bands.

As for the players, they travelled down a day or two ahead of the match, and stayed in a country house near to the ground. On the sunny morning before the game, Jimmy Catton visited the house and found Andy Aitken sitting outside on a lawn chair with a stack of foolscap paper in his lap. 'This was covered in writing,' said Catton, 'and he confided to me that he was learning by heart the speech he was to deliver when he received the cup.' This was not necessarily bravado on Aitken's part. He dreaded public speaking – 'He had no ambition to be an orator,' said Catton – and it was probably more down to nerves. Catton was a big fan of 'the Daddler', who he considered to be one of the finest 'middlemen' the game had ever seen. In the end, though, Aitken's speech would never be delivered.

At the Crystal Palace, as the big match got underway, the huge crowd strained to get the best possible view of the action. 'In the trees – elm, oak, spruce, plane, beech and even holly – they clung like crows,' said the *Mirror*. 'They swarmed up the telegraph poles. They straddled the roof of the telegraph office. They looted every plank and ladder in the grounds and improvised stands. They dragged refreshment tables from tents and stood on marble tops.' Some fans resorted to standing on upturned ginger beer bottles, desperate to catch a glimpse of the action.

Back at home, fans relied on updates sent by telegraph wires and carrier pigeons. In Newcastle, a network of 37 newsagent shops received ten-minute bulletins circulated by cyclists. Supporters crowded around the shops as updates were pasted in windows. Pigeon fanciers stood outside the newsagents with their birds in paper bags, sending them home with score updates for villages and towns across the region. 'Thanks to the perfect organisation of the *Daily Mirror*, the result was known in Newcastle within a minute of the finish of play,' the paper modestly explained.

For the Geordies, though, the result wasn't worth waiting for. Despite being favourites to win, Newcastle were comprehensively outplayed by an excellent Aston Villa side. Villa took the lead after just three minutes through a Harry Hampton header, and then restricted Newcastle to long-range shots. Just before half-time, Bill Appleyard smashed a shot from distance against the Villa post.

The second half was very physical, with Jack Rutherford earning a black eye, and Jimmy Lawrence being knocked out cold by a shoulder charge from Hampton. With no substitutes, a revived Lawrence had to play on. He played brilliantly, too, and made a remarkable save low down at his post, only to see his defenders fail to clear the rebound, allowing Hampton to score again, securing Villa a 2-0 win.

The Newcastle fans at the Palace were full of grace after the match. 'The Geordies took their reverse with "canny" composure,' said the *Mirror*. It had, after all, been a first attempt to win the cup final, and there would always be next year. In the meantime, there was a league campaign to finish. As the defeated Newcastle team returned home, they were greeted by an appreciative crowd that filled Central Station and lined its approaches. A grateful Andy Aitken told them he was confident his team would not lose a point in the league and would win the championship.

In the penultimate league match of the season, Newcastle went to Sheffield to play The Wednesday and won 3-1. That left the Magpies a point behind leaders Everton and level with Man City. Everton had already played their final game, Man City had to play cup winners Aston Villa, and Newcastle had to play Middlesbrough, at Ayresome Park. Newcastle's superior goal average meant that a win would secure the championship.

United were without the injured Andy McCombie, Alec Gardner and Peter McWilliam. Bill McCracken and Newcastle-born reserve team forward Ted McIntyre deputised, and Ron Orr, who had missed the cup final, returned to the side. Perhaps stung by the cup final defeat, and determined not to fail again, Newcastle went for the jugular from the kick-off, peppering the Middlesbrough goal with shots. Ron Orr gave the Magpies the lead after just five minutes, but 'superb defence' from Boro kept the score down. Early in the second half, Rutherford beat two defenders and the keeper to score a 'grand' goal. Within a minute of the restart, Appleyard ran through the defence to score a third 'great goal'. The match finished 3-0 to Newcastle.

'The Tyneside club's followers were loud in their expressions of delight,' said one report, perhaps understating the celebrations that followed. Another report described 'a scene of enthusiasm as is seldom witnessed on a football ground'. Elsewhere, Man City lost to Villa, but that result had become irrelevant. Newcastle United had won the Football League, as the *Penny Illustrated* put it, 'in somewhat sensational style.' It was a thoroughly deserved triumph. The *Mirror* said Newcastle were 'well worthy of the "best side of the year",' and 'the most popular winners of the league trophy in recent years.' Newcastle United - League Champions 1904/05. The club had won its first major honour.

The team's reception at Central Station on the return from Middlesbrough that evening was 'one to remember'. As the special train pulled into the station the cheering began, 'and continued without intermission for some ten minutes'. They were driven in a brake through 'an enormous crowd' to be greeted by the mayor at the Palace Theatre on Percy Street. 'The number of people in the line of route was the greatest seen in Newcastle for years,' wrote one reporter. At the theatre, the team and staff were invited onto the stage to receive applause, but 'Captain Aitken could not be induced to burst into speech'. This was a man who preferred to do his talking on the pitch, and he had quietly kept his promise to Newcastle fans by winning the league.

Walking along Percy Street today, towards the site of the Palace Theatre, much has changed since Edwardian times, although there are a few remaining familiarities. The team's brake would have passed by the Three Bulls Heads pub, which exists in the same location – although in a modernised building – today. Further along, it would have rolled past the Percy Arms and the Hotspur, again both of which are still there today. The Palace Theatre itself, which stood at the junction of Percy Street and St Thomas Street was demolished in 1961. In its place are three prefabs containing a bookmakers, a dry cleaners, and a charity shop. Above their low roofs you can see the St James' Park stands pointing to the sky.

The fact that the enormous crowd that lined the route was 'the greatest seen in Newcastle for years' demonstrates how much the football club was beginning to matter to the city and its population as a whole, and not just to the 22,000 or so who regularly paid their sixpence at St James' Park. These players had represented Newcastle on a national stage, and they'd come home victorious. Reward for their victory came in the form of the silver Football League Championship trophy, nicknamed 'The Lady' due to the small female figure that stands on the lid.

Although the league celebrations were abundant, and thoroughly deserved, there must have been a hint of disappointment. At the time, the FA Cup was a much greater prize than the league championship. The league, after all, was simply an organised means of playing regular games in order to generate a regular income. The FA Cup, on the other hand, was football's oldest and most prestigious competition, drawing bigger attendances and meriting wider newspaper coverage.

The FA Cup was regarded as more important than the league for the majority of football's history, arguably right up to the inception of the Premier League in 1992. Certainly in the Edwardian era a team could not be considered the best in the country until it had won football's biggest prize. So Newcastle's players and staff enjoyed winning the league, then immediately set their sights on winning the cup.

Newcastle United 1905/06 team postcard
With 1904/05 Football League trophy. In kit, left to right; back
row: Andy McCombie, Jimmy Lawrence; third row: Jack Carr,
Bill McCracken, Peter McWilliam, Joe McClarence; second row:
Andy Aitken, Jack Rutherford, Jimmy Howie, Bill Appleyard,
Ron Orr, Bert Gosnell; front row: Colin Veitch, Alec Gardner

Colin Veitch, Andy Aitken and Jack Rutherford,
Singleton & Cole's Footballers cigarette cards, 1905

Colin Veitch Ogden's
cigarette card, 1908

Overleaf:
Taddy & Co 'Prominent
Footballers' Newcastle United
cigarette card collection, 1907
From a huge first set of 595
cards issued by James Taddy
& Co, one of the most prolific
and important publishers of
cigarette cards

PROMINENT FOOTBALLERS.

A. McCOMBIE,
NEWCASTLE UNITED.

PROMINENT FOOTBALLERS.

W. McCRACKEN,
NEWCASTLE UNITED.

PROMINENT FOOTBALLERS.

J. LAWRENCE.
NEWCASTLE UNITED

PROMINENT FOOTBALLERS.

J. CARR,
NEWCASTLE UNITED.

PROMINENT FOOTBALLERS.

P. McWILLIAM,
NEWCASTLE UNITED.

PROMINENT FOOTBALLERS.

C. VEITCH,
NEWCASTLE UNITED.

PROMINENT FOOTBALLERS.

A. GARDNER,
NEWCASTLE UNITED.

PROMINENT FOOTBALLERS.

F. SPEEDIE,
NEWCASTLE UNITED.

PROMINENT FOOTBALLERS.

J. HOWIE,
NEWCASTLE UNITED.

PROMINENT FOOTBALLERS.

W. APPLEYARD,
NEWCASTLE UNITED.

PROMINENT FOOTBALLERS.

J. RUTHERFORD.
NEWCASTLE UNITED.

PROMINENT FOOTBALLERS.

R. ORR,
NEWCASTLE UNITED.

St James' Park, taken from Leazes Terrace during a Newcastle vs Sunderland FA Cup tie that ended 2-2, 6 March 1909

'Outside Newcastle United's football ground after the match' taken from Barrack Road/Gallowgate c.1909

10

Football Magicians

In front of me is a cigarette card, a tiny piece of football history, just a couple of inches tall. The card was issued by the Singleton & Cole's cigarette company in 1905 as part of its superb 'Footballers' collection. Cigarette cards were hugely popular with football fans, combining as they did the twin delights of the round ball game and smoking. The cards were inserted into flimsy cigarette packs to protect their contents, and from the 1880s manufacturers printed pictures on them – of birds, flowers and, inevitably, footballers. The Singleton & Cole's set was one of the first to feature the head and shoulder shots of footballers that have been familiar on football cards and stickers ever since.

This card is number 22 out of 50. It would be nice to say it had been lovingly cared for and handed down through several generations of my family, but it was actually bought on eBay late one night after several cold drinks. The slightly-worn card depicts a handsome young man, clean shaven, side-parted hair brushed into a slight quiff. He is wears a black and white-striped shirt that hangs low around his neck, buttons fastened tightly at his chest. He leans forward slightly, with a pensive look on his face, and gazes past the camera, apparently caught in his thoughts.

It's a striking image, and it seems immediately obvious that the man depicted is someone special, someone out of the ordinary. Singleton & Cole's 'Footballers' number 22 is C Veitch of Newcastle United. He is arguably the greatest player in the club's history.

Colin Campbell McKechnie Veitch was born in Newcastle in the same year as his football club – 1881. His family lived at 133 Byker Bank, not far from the early Stanley Street and East End grounds. He was the youngest of four brothers, and his dad was a relieving officer whose work involved admitting the poor to the local workhouse. Young Colin excelled at football from an early age, and played for Newcastle Schools. On one occasion, in 1894, he scored a goal against Sunderland Schools at St James' Park. He was a big lad for his age, and it's said that his teachers carried copies of his birth certificate so they could prove to opposition teams he was eligible to play. He subsequently played for Rutherford College, while continuing his studies with the aim of becoming a school teacher.

However, his talents had been spotted by Newcastle United. He played in trial games for the club, and signed up as an amateur, also playing for the reserve team under the pseudonym 'Hamilton' – an indication that Newcastle prized this young player and didn't want him being poached by anyone else. When he turned 18 in 1899, Veitch was offered a professional contract. Perhaps surprisingly, he was reluctant to sign. As well as a desire to become a teacher, he had a strong interest in politics, and in particular the socialist movement. Did he really want to be a professional footballer, rather than dedicating himself to more cerebral pursuits? Obviously, he decided that he did.

The earliest photograph to be found of Colin Veitch is a team shot from 1898/99 showing the Newcastle United 'A' reserve side, winners that season of the Northumberland Cup and the Northern Alliance. The photograph is fairly typical of team shots in which Veitch appears, in that he looks very out of place. As in the cigarette card photo, he is not looking at the camera, but staring off to the side somewhere, seemingly lost once again in his thoughts. He has no Victorian moustache, no grease-flattened hair. He looks entirely modern, and appears so detached and so different to those around him that it seems almost like he has been Photoshopped in from the 21st century. He appears to be a man out of his time. In many ways he was ahead of his time, and that served Newcastle very well over the course of his long association with the club.

Veitch made his first team debut in October 1899, and filled in as a utility man in various different positions over the next couple of seasons, scoring a handful of goals. He was incredibly versatile. Primarily a half-back, or central midfielder, he played all over the pitch for Newcastle, including at centre-forward. Perhaps as a result of his versatility, Veitch didn't become a regular until the 1903/04 season, when he was 22.

That was the season in which Newcastle, under the tutelage of Bob McColl, began to develop their highly effective 'combination' passing style. Young Veitch was quickly sold on the idea. Like McColl and Andy Aitken, Veitch was a thinker, an 'intelligent footballer'. He was one of the few players consulted by the committee over team selection and, with Bill McCracken, he devised the club's ruthlessly effective offside trap. Veitch was tough, too – rare film footage of him in action demonstrates that he was just as likely to use his shoulder to knock an opponent onto their backside as he was to use his brain to pick out a pass. But he appreciated the 'scientific' Scottish game, and understood that short passing and possession were the keys to unleashing decisive attacking plays.

When Newcastle won the league for the first time in 1904/05, Veitch played in six different positions and contributed ten goals. He's pictured lounging under the league trophy in the following season's team photo. It's an odd arrangement, his teammates sitting behind him, arms folded, while Veitch lies, propped on one elbow, like a teenager in front of the TV on a living room carpet. He'd move closer to the middle of the team photo in subsequent seasons, becoming integral to the team, and central to its success.

In 1905/06 Newcastle set out with the express intention to win football's greatest prize, the one they had so narrowly missed out on in the previous season – the FA Cup. The season began at a completely remodelled St James's Park, which boasted a doubled capacity of 60,000. The pitch was improved, and the open terraces had been enlarged. Central to the redevelopment was a brand new barrel-roofed corrugated steel and timber West Stand, built to seat 4,600 fans at a cost of £8,000. Many modern

Newcastle fans will be familiar with this Edwardian West Stand. It stood for a remarkable 82 years, before being demolished in 1987.

Journalist Charles Sutcliffe wrote in the *Daily Express* about the club's ambitions. 'Newcastle is a great sporting town, and the United club is governed by a management that is simply boundless in its ambitious aims,' he wrote. 'Such are the aspirations of the Newcastle directors that the world "modesty" is not to be found in their vocabulary. They are simply mad in their desire to be caretakers of the Football Association Challenge Cup.'

Such focus on the cup appeared to be to the detriment of the club's league campaign. The reigning league champions won only one of their first seven league matches. The ship was steadied ahead of the Tyne-Wear derby in December 1905, at which the ground's new capacity was tested by a massive 56,000-strong crowd – the biggest that had ever watched a football match in Newcastle. Ron Orr scored for the Magpies in a 1-1 draw.

In the end, despite claims that they did not care 'the toss of a button' about the league competition, Newcastle finished in a thoroughly respectable fourth place. Meanwhile, their focus on the FA Cup saw them beat Grimsby, Derby, Blackpool, Birmingham and then, in the semi-finals, Woolwich Arsenal. Newcastle were going back to the Crystal Palace, to play in a second successive FA Cup final, this time against Everton.

If anything, excitement on Tyneside was even greater than it had been in the previous season. Those who had travelled to London for the first final were determined to do so again, and those who had heard tales from the capital were determined to join them. Pits and factories set up cup final funds to help workers pay for their trips, and clubs and churches organised excursions to London for their members. Throughout the day before the match, trains and charabancs left Newcastle packed with hundreds of fans. Thousands more travelled on overnight excursions. Central Station was rammed with travellers, and with family and friends who had gathered to wave them off. And this wasn't just a boys' day out. The *Daily Mirror* reported that 'the feature of the whole day was the unusual number of ladies travelling.'

'The cup fever had a large hold on Newcastle,' said the *Mirror*, 'and many of those walking in the streets with no intention of journeying to London wore black and white ties and hat bands, or wore rosettes of the favourite magpie colours.'

It was set to be the 'match of the season', and Newcastle were regarded as favourites. They were missing the increasingly-injured Bill Appleyard, but Ron Orr was considered an able deputy. Ultimately, though, it was a disappointing game, 'a dull, dismal display', featuring 'the worst play for years', and 'a poor show to bring people many miles to see'. The game was decided by a single goal, scored with a quarter of an hour left to play by Everton's Sandy Young. Newcastle had lost their second successive FA Cup final.

'Newcastle received the news of United's defeat with amazement,' reported Charles Sutcliffe. 'Disappointment was again the lot of the United's supporters.' At this point, many modern Newcastle fans will be able to very easily empathise with their Edwardian counterparts. The club did, of course, lose two consecutive FA Cup finals in the modern era, in 1998 and 1999.

As for the team, the best compliment Sutcliffe could find was that 'Lawrence was free from blame'. 'They lacked everything that the team have shown themselves masters of. It may be stage fright or nervousness, but clearly the United can have no love for the Palace.'

In the following season, ironically, it was the Crystal Palace club rather than the Crystal Palace ground that caused Newcastle an FA Cup nightmare. The modern incarnation of Crystal Palace FC had formed only a year earlier, and initially played at the Crystal Palace ground. But it was at St James' Park, in the very first round, that Palace dumped Newcastle out of the cup, beating the Magpies 1-0 in front of 30,000 disconsolate fans.

With the cup off the agenda for another season, the club was at least free to concentrate on the league. They opened the 1906/07 season with a 4-2 win over Sunderland in front of 56,875 – the highest attendance St James' Park had ever seen. Over the course of the season, Newcastle's average attendance reached almost 34,000, confirming its position as the best-supported club in the country.

There was one big change on the pitch this season. Andy Aitken, the Daddler, lost his place at half-back to the increasingly-influential Colin Veitch. Still only 30, and still a Scotland international, Aitken was too good a player to sit on the sidelines at Newcastle. He left in November 1906, moving to Middlesbrough to become player-manager. Aitken had made over 300 appearances for Newcastle. As well as being a truly great player, he'd been a leader and an innovator, helping to implement the club's effective passing style. He'd also been a winner, leading his side to the Football League Championship, and becoming the first Newcastle United captain to lift a major trophy. Newcastle remained in his heart. He ran a couple of pubs in the city – the White Hart Inn in the Cloth Market and the Douglas Hotel on Grainger Street – and he lived on Tyneside after his career ended, up until his death, aged 77, in 1955.

With the great Andy Aitken gone, the soon-to-be greater Colin Veitch took centre stage. Veitch was now an integral part of the first team, and he increasingly began to pull the strings. He had clear ideas about how the game should be played, adapting Bob McColl's passing game, keen to make it slicker and more productive. He instigated 'round table conferences', essentially team meetings to discuss plans and strategies, which were practically unheard of in football at the time. It's thought that Veitch was the first man to bring a blackboard into a football dressing room in order to set out tactics.

Bob Hewison, who would succeed Veitch at half-back for Newcastle, wrote in 1914 about Veitch's influence on the club's style of play. He called the style 'the sixth forward game', wherein a half-back (usually Veitch himself) supported five forward players in pursuit of 'pure football' and 'goals, goals, goals'. Hewison wrote: 'His football was a result of his brains. He it was who developed the sixth forward game to such perfection so far as Newcastle United were concerned – a game which earned for that club the title of football magicians, carpet weavers, scientists, football machines etc.'

Veitch's 'football magicians' enjoyed a spellbinding league season, turning St James' Park into an invincible fortress. Newcastle won every single home game right up to the last one of the season, against Sheffield United. Another win would have secured the league title for the Magpies. But, without Appleyard, McCracken or Gardner, they could only manage a goalless draw. Fortunately, however, league rivals Everton lost at Derby, handing the title to the Magpies.

That made it two league championships within three seasons for Newcastle, a feat that seems difficult to comprehend for a modern fan so starved of success. They won another trophy, too – the Sheriff of London Charity Shield. Newcastle took on top amateur team Corinthians at Craven Cottage, and beat them 5-2. At this rate, the club was going to have to build a trophy cabinet. But they had still to win football's biggest prize.

So, with Newcastle now widely regarded as the best team in the county, focus for the 1907/08 season shifted again towards winning the FA Cup. This resulted in an uneven league campaign, during which Newcastle were beaten at home by Sunderland, but beat their rivals away, were thumped 6-1 by Manchester United, but thrashed Birmingham City 8-0.

There was one other remarkable scoreline during the 1907/08 season, in a friendly match on Anglesey. Newcastle were on a winter tour of North Wales, and the opposition was a local side called Beaumaris. The final score was 14-1 to Newcastle, with big Bill Appleyard scoring a triple hat-trick of nine goals, equalling Alec White's great feat against Point Pleasant back in 1888.

But the main talking point of the season was another great cup run, with Newcastle thrashing Fulham 6-0 in the semi at neutral Anfield to once again reach the FA Cup final. It was a return to the dreaded Crystal Palace, but surely this would prove third time lucky – particularly as the opposition were second division Wolves. United were clear favourites, and had no real injury concerns. They prepared for the final in relaxed fashion, bathing in the salt baths at Saltburn. Unfortunately, their preparations were fruitless once again.

Newcastle started the final brightly, but team captain Alec Gardner missed a couple of chances 'in wretched fashion'. Then, five minutes before half-time, a 25-yard shot from Wolves' ecclesiastical right-half Reverend Kenneth Hunt was inexplicably fumbled over the line by Jimmy Lawrence. Disastrously, three minutes later, George Hedley brushed off Bill McCracken to fire in a second. Newcastle were 2-0 down at half-time.

In the second half, Newcastle pushed forward, with Colin Veitch 'resplendent and argumentative' in attack. With a quarter of an hour left, Jimmy Howie pulled a goal back. It was Newcastle's first goal at the Crystal Palace in three visits. Despite attempts to grab an equaliser, they couldn't increase that tally. Billy Harrison beat the Newcastle defence to make the score 3-1 to Wolves, and that's how the match ended.

'It is no use; they cannot win the cup,' wrote Charles Sutcliffe. 'Newcastle United have for the third time failed unexpectedly, if not ignominiously.' Sutcliffe praised the half-back line of Gardner, Veitch and McWilliam, but was scathing of the rest of the team, particularly Appleyard, who he said 'was only seen in failure'. The big striker was also singled out for blame by the club's directors. He'd scored 88 goals over five seasons, but he would never play for Newcastle again.

After the match, Colin Veitch joked that the FA should buy a new cup, 'then Newcastle might have a chance.' A disappointed Alec Gardner said, 'Well, our turn will surely come someday.' So the loss was put down to sheer bad luck. A *Daily Mirror* reporter wrote, 'For a side to reach the final three times in four years and yet not reap the fruits of victory is indeed hard Cheddar.'

Newcastle's defeat was met with disbelief by many. Journalist Jimmy Catton called Newcastle 'the most extraordinary team who ever tried to win the cup at the Crystal Palace.' 'Newcastle were the riddle of the fields,' he wrote. 'Their football could be superb, and perfectly beautiful. No man could wish for anything more crafty and skilful. Yet they were overawed by the Palace.'

Some said the team had suffered from nerves, and simply could not cope with the pressure of a cup final. Certainly the demands of the club's growing fanbase, and the associated expectations in their home city, must have registered in the players' minds. It's a question that's still occasionally raised in the modern era – does the burden of expectation from the fans weigh too heavily on the players' shoulders? Is that why Newcastle United perennially struggle to win anything? Because it matters too much to too many? In 1908, Colin Veitch said that wasn't true. The players hadn't been nervous, he said, the implication being that they had simply performed poorly, and been outplayed.

There was also talk of a Crystal Palace 'curse', and certainly it seemed that Newcastle could not buy a win on the national field. They'd now lost three FA Cup finals at the Palace, but that may have been less to do with a curse, and more to do with the fact that the Crystal Palace pitch was entirely different to any other in English football. Due to its location within a natural basin in the Sydenham park, it managed to retain moisture and remained lush. While other pitches had their surfaces worn bare and hard by regular training and matches, the Crystal Palace pitch remained green and soft. It was more like a golf fairway than a football pitch. The verdant surface just didn't suit Newcastle's close-passing game. They were used to pinging the ball around over bare mud surfaces, and struggled when the game was slowed down by thick grass.

Newcastle fans who had travelled to London had plenty of time on the return journey to chew over the defeat, or to consider more proactive things. Gladstone Adams, a Newcastle supporter and professional photographer from Whitley Bay, had driven down to the Crystal Palace in his new-fangled motor car, an imported French Darracq. On the way back, he was caught in an April hail shower, which obscured his sheet glass windscreen, and forced him to keep stopping to clear it. The experience inspired Gladstone to invent and patent something that is an essential feature of every modern car – the windscreen wiper.

There are a few other Colin Veitch cigarette cards in this collection. Two of them, from Cope's 'Clips' and John Sinclair, feature an identical photograph, an angled headshot showing Veitch with hands folded tightly under his armpits and hair carefully greased into an impressively-tall quiff. Another, from Ogden's and dating from 1908, features a brightly-coloured illustration of Veitch, with blue eyes, brown hair and rosy cheeks, forward-facing, arms folded, broad shoulders cropped by the edges of the card. On the back of the Odgen's card is a short profile. 'The centre-half for Newcastle United has been such an excellent utility man that this has led to him being chosen as reserve for international games, instead of being given a definite place,' it says. 'He holds five international caps, however.' Veitch had won his first cap against Ireland in 1906, but would only win one further cap after the publication of this cigarette card, taking his total to just six, a figure that doesn't begin to reflect his talent.

For the next season, 1908/09, Veitch was appointed club captain, and Newcastle signed his sometime England colleague, inside-forward Jimmy 'Tadger' Stewart. Bill Appleyard was replaced at centre-forward by Bob Blanthorne from Grimsby Town. But disaster struck on this tall and 'very clever' player's debut, against Bradford City at St James' Park. Blanthorne collided with Bradford left-back Fred Farren and suffered a severe leg break. He was out of action for 18 months, and never played for the first team again, eventually being sold to Hartlepools United.

Newcastle fared pretty well without a centre-forward, with Veitch and Jimmy Howie in great goalscoring form as they won their first seven home games of the season. However, in their eighth game they were beaten 2-0 by Aston Villa, and part of the St James' Park crowd turned on the players. Many supporters were still smarting from the FA Cup final embarrassment(s), and, never shy to voice their opinions, they used this lacklustre performance to vent their anger. Footballers had yet to be deified by their public, and support had to be earned. Fans just wouldn't allow their players to let them down.

There were ructions behind the scenes, too, and the club committee responded by dropping Howie, McCracken, McWilliam, Rutherford and Stewart – all international players. The club also went out and bought a new centre-forward, Albert Shepherd from Bolton Wanderers, for the 'exceptionally high fee' of £850. Newspapers called Shepherd 'the best centre-forward in the country'. He'd made one appearance for England, and had scored on his international debut. And he scored on his Newcastle debut, as the new-look United team went to Nottingham Forest and won 4-0. But disaster struck in the next match – at home to Sunderland.

It was 'baff Saturday', the day after miners received their two-weekly pay, and that helped swell the crowd to more than 56,000. Jimmy Catton travelled to Newcastle to watch the match, but arrived late and found the gates locked. Pushing through crowds outside the club's offices, he spotted Frank Watt. 'Frank! Frank!' he yelled. Watt recognised the journalist. 'What are you doing there, man?' he said. 'Make way for this gentleman!' Unfortunately, there were no spare seats in the ground, so Watt fetched a chair from the office and placed it at the touchline for Catton to watch this remarkable Tyne-Wear derby at close range. 'The tremendous rivalry always enthralled me,' said Catton. 'The vast crowd simply buzzed with the pleasure of anticipation and the burr of the Northumbrian throng.'

It was quite a game, and one that would be remembered for the wrong reasons on Tyneside. Sunderland scored first, but Newcastle equalised just before half-time through a Shepherd penalty. Sunderland claimed that the penalty – given for handball – should not have stood, and their anger most likely fuelled what happened next. 'What Sunderland said or resolved in their dressing room I cannot say, but events proved they were smarting under a sense of injustice,' wrote Catton. 'They expressed their feelings in a way which was most disastrous to the reputation of Newcastle.'

In the second half, Sunderland simply battered Newcastle, scoring eight goals in less than half an hour. The full-time score was 9-1. It was a hugely embarrassing result. It's fair to assume that the St James' Park crowd gave the players a verbal ticking-off. The stick that Edwardian Geordies must have received from Sunderland-supporting work colleagues does not bear thinking about.

However, the huge embarrassment caused by this fateful result might well have been the kick up the backside that was required to propel Newcastle towards more glory. The five dropped internationals were restored to the team, and the Magpies went on a storming run, winning 13 of their next 15 games. That was enough to push them to the top of the league table.

In the FA Cup, Newcastle gained some form of revenge on Sunderland, winning 3-0 at Roker to knock the Wearsiders out of the cup in a storm of sleet and rain. And the Magpies avoided having to deal with the Crystal

Palace curse this season – by being beaten 1-0 by Manchester United in the semi-final at Bramall Lane. There would be no cup final for the Magpies in 1908/09.

Back in the league, Newcastle continued their great form, seeing off rivals Blackburn, The Wednesday and Woolwich Arsenal. And the club's third league championship was secured with five games still to play, courtesy of a 3-0 win over nearest challengers Everton. Tadger Stewart scored two, and Bill McCracken scored a rare goal, from the penalty spot. Newcastle had won the league with a then-record 53 points, seven points clear of Everton.

It was another fantastic triumph for the Magpies, which at the time probably wasn't properly appreciated. Newspaper coverage afforded to the league win was perfunctory. After all, Newcastle had already proven they could win the league. By way of gauging supporter interest, 30,000 watched the league-clinching win over Everton, while more than 40,000 watched the cup run-ending defeat to Manchester United. It was the FA Cup that people were most bothered about.

Newcastle's third league championship win was also a third win for Colin Veitch – and his first as captain. Away from the pitch, Veitch, along with his good mate Jimmy Lawrence, had become involved with the Association Football Players Union (AFPU). He wrote articles for the *Union* newspaper, and played a key role when a major dispute erupted between the AFPU and the FA in 1909.

The dispute centred around compensation payments for injured players. The AFPU wanted to take cases where clubs refused to pay compensation to court. The FA said that such cases should be dealt with under their authority, and should not be taken to court. The two parties disagreed, and the FA ceased to recognise the union. The FA then ordered all players to resign from the AFPU, otherwise they would have their professional registrations cancelled. Many players did resign, but others refused, notably many of Veitch's Newcastle teammates, several members of the Sunderland squad, and the entire Manchester United squad, led by Veitch's friend Billy Meredith.

With the FA refusing to speak to the 'militant' Meredith, Veitch attempted to negotiate on the players' behalf. Adopting a conciliatory stance, he argued successfully for a truce. Although both sides were forced to compromise, Veitch called it 'peace with honour'. Jimmy Catton said of Veitch, 'The players have never had a man of such vision and suave power.' The truce came at a cost, though. Like others who had stood up to the FA, Veitch was never picked for England again.

The Veitch cigarette cards are wonderful, but there are other favourites, including a very youthful Jimmy Lawrence, an only slightly less youthful Bill McCracken (who looks a little like a young George Harrison), a stern-faced and centre-parted Jack Carr, a side-parted and arms-folded Jack Rutherford, a baby-faced Peter McWilliam, a smiling, jug-eared Jimmy Howie, and a very sombre-looking Albert Shepherd. Shuffling these cards around on a table top, we can begin to build a team that would go on to achieve unprecedented glory as perhaps the greatest Newcastle United side of all time.

Albert Shepherd
F&J Smith Footballers
cigarette card, c.1911

Father and son
Newcastle fans at the
1910 FA Cup Final

Stuart and Winfield.]
W. McCRACKEN
(*Newcastle United*).

Stuart and Winfield.]
LAWRENCE
(*Newcastle*).

Bill McCracken and Jimmy Lawrence,
from The Book of Football

Newcastle United 'Winners of the English Cup 1909-10' card
The team is finally pictured with the old FA Cup, left to right;
back row: Bill McCracken, Wilf Low, Albert Shepherd, Peter
McWilliam, Jack Carr; middle: Jack Rutherford, Jimmy Howie,
Colin Veitch, Sandy Higgins, George Wilson, Tony Whitson;
front: Frank Watt, Jimmy Lawrence, Jimmy McPherson

11

The Cup

It's an unavoidable fact that Newcastle United's greatest days are buried long in the past. To enjoy them requires a delve into history, and a strong reliance on yellowed newspaper columns. There is now no one left alive who is old enough to remember Newcastle's glorious Edwardian era. But there are a few surviving items that can help to transport us back to those days, a few pieces of evidence that can help us understand and appreciate the long-ago achievements of this football club. There is one item in particular I'm very keen to see, and to find it I'm off on the train to Manchester and the National Football Museum.

The Urbis building is a striking sight to the north of Manchester's city centre. The wedge-shaped building was designed as part of a regeneration project following the IRA bombing in 1996. Opened in 2002, it was originally an exhibition centre, before becoming the permanent home of the National Football Museum in 2012. Today, the building's glass sides gleam in the sun, its crooked spire pointing towards the city below. Banners along the approach to the museum promise *drama, history, skill, art, faith, style, passion, football.*

Heading into the museum, I stop to buy a visitor's guide, then pass through the turnstile entrance. This really is a brilliant place, recognising that what is special about football is the stuff that's been around for years, and presenting an accessible and entertaining history of the game through photos, memorabilia, films and inter-active displays. If you love football and have any interest in its history, this is pretty much a perfect place to be.

On the ground floor, a big open space below mezzanine levels, is the Hall of Fame. Newcastle is well-represented. Former players Jackie Milburn, Len Shackleton, Kevin Keegan, Peter Beardsley, Paul Gascoigne and Alan Shearer have all been inducted, as has former manager Sir Bobby Robson. What's striking is the fact that of these undoubted heroes, only Milburn actually won anything for the club. Even our greatest stars have struggled for silverware. None of Newcastle's Edwardian stars have been inducted. Not yet, anyway.

By 1910, Newcastle had won the Football League three times. That was impressive, and it was enough to secure the club a reputation as one of the best of the Edwardian era. But the league was of secondary importance, and the real prize was the FA Cup. Newcastle had lost three FA Cup finals, in 1905, 1906 and 1908, each time at the Crystal Palace, a seemingly cursed venue that was hated by Geordie fans. The club went into the 1909/10 season as league champions, but for secretary Frank Watt, trainer Jimmy McPherson and captain Colin Veitch the focus was not on retaining the league title but on finally winning the cup.

There had been a handful of changes to the squad. Most notably, the club had lost the services of the great right-half Alec Gardner. He suffered a broken leg in a cup tie at Blackpool in February 1909, and never played for the club again. Gardner had made more than 300 appearances for the Magpies, and played in all three league-winning sides. He'd captained the side during the victorious 1906-07 season. Although relatively unsung among the club's Edwardian heroes, Gardner was hugely popular at the time with fans, who would call in to talk football with him at his pub, the Dun Cow Inn, which was near to the Hancock Museum.

Andy McCombie was still at the club but had retired from playing, and now worked as an assistant to trainer Jimmy McPherson. McCombie would remain involved with Newcastle for more than 40 years – not bad for a player who had been signed from Sunderland. And forward Ron Orr, who had scored 70 goals for the Magpies, was now at Liverpool. Orr had been criticised by fans after missing chances in big matches, but he'd soon get the chance to remind them of what he could do.

So Newcastle went into the 1909/10 season with a first-choice team that consisted of Jimmy Lawrence in goal, and Bill McCracken at the back, partnered by South African-born and Newcastle-raised Tony Whitson. Whitson had worked his way up through the club's ranks, but had found opportunities limited with McCombie and Jack Carr ahead of him. But with McCombie retired and Carr now 33, Whitson got his chance. He'd go on to make almost 150 appearances for the Magpies.

At half-back, Colin Veitch and Peter McWilliam were

joined by Wilf Low, signed from Aberdeen for £800. Low was nicknamed 'the Laughing Cavalier', despite the stern look he adopts in photographs, and his hard-hitting playing style. Tom Coulthard wrote in the *Chronicle* that Low was 'grim in his methods and fearless to the point of grave risk to himself in the headlong dive for the ball that he often employed'.

Up front, alongside Jack Rutherford, Jimmy Howie and Albert Shepherd were two players who had established themselves during the previous season, Sandy Higgins and George Wilson. Alex 'Sandy' Higgins was a skilful left-footer who scored plenty of goals from inside-left, and also filled in at centre-forward. He was the son of another Alex 'Sandy' Higgins, who played for Derby County and Nottingham Forest. And outside-left George Wilson was another of Newcastle's tricky little wingers, signed from Everton after a bust-up with the Toffees' board. Both Scottish internationals, Higgins and Wilson had long careers at Newcastle, and chipped in with some very important goals.

Although the focus was on the cup, 1909/10 was a decent league season for Newcastle. They beat Sunderland home and away, scored 70 goals in 38 games, and ended up finishing fourth. The most extraordinary league game of the season was played at Liverpool's Anfield in December 1909. Jimmy Howie gave Newcastle the lead, only for Liverpool to quickly equalise. Then Albert Shepherd took centre stage, scoring four goals in swift succession, with Liverpool replying once more, to make the score 5-2 to Newcastle at half-time.

Liverpool's former-Newcastle secretary Tom Watson

was so annoyed that he locked himself in his office and refused to watch the second half. That was a mistake on his behalf. Liverpool scored four goals – two of them from former Newcastle hero Ron Orr – and ended up winning 6-5. 'Never in the history of the Newcastle club have they been three goals to the good at the interval and been defeated in the second half,' wrote a reporter for the *Hull Daily Mail*. 'Football is, and always will be, a game of glorious uncertainty.'

Newcastle needed a replay to see off Stoke in the first round of the cup, then comfortably won home ties against Fulham, Blackburn Rovers and Leicester Fosse. The club was criticised for prioritising cup ties over league fixtures, an approach that saw them rest key players. However, that can probably be excused when you consider that, for example, they were fixtured to play Woolwich Arsenal in the league on a Friday evening, then Swindon Town in the FA Cup semi-final on the Saturday afternoon.

The semi was played at White Hart Lane, and Newcastle had no qualms about making the trip – they'd beaten Spurs 4-0 there the week before. The Magpies travelled without centre-forward Albert Shepherd. He'd been barracked by fans (one report says he was 'hissed') for his 'very erratic' performance during the Arsenal league match on the previous day, and had walked from the field, telling the referee he was leaving 'as a protest against the conduct of the crowd'. He was, unsurprisingly, dropped for the cup game. Tadger Stewart filled in against Swindon, and scored. Jack Rutherford also scored in a 2-0 win. Newcastle were heading back to the Crystal

Palace. Their cup final opponents would be mid-table second division side Barnsley. Surely the cup jinx could finally be overturned?

Here in Manchester, the first floor of the museum is a football fanatic's paradise. The origins of the game are tracked via some fascinating exhibits, including blown bladder balls, the FA's 1863 minute book containing the original Laws of the Game, and a winner's medal from the first FA Cup final in 1872. There are boots and books, rosettes and cigarette cards, match programmes and ticket stubs. An interactive display provides information on the formation of clubs, even if that information is not always accurate. ('Newcastle United was formed in 1892...' For shame, National Football Museum!) Most impressive are the collections of match worn shirts, and cabinets full of trophies – one of particular significance.

The Newcastle team headed down to London on the day before the cup final, and Albert Shepherd was on the train. He'd had a tough time, having been relegated to the reserves following his behaviour during the Arsenal game – an act for which he was fined £5. Club officials had intended to leave him out for the final, but his teammates had threatened to strike if he wasn't included. Despite missing a total of ten matches, Shepherd had still scored 29 goals over the season, and the players knew they couldn't win the cup without him.

The supporters followed the team down to the capital on the Saturday morning, their trains given a 'hearty send-off' by crowds of well-wishers. The fans, in their flat caps and bowlers, packed into the carriages for the long, slow journey south. Some wore black and white rosettes, and one chap and his young son, later pictured in newspapers, wore matching black and white-striped coats, trousers, boots and top hats, and twirled black and white walking canes. Meanwhile, the good folk of Barnsley were also heading for the capital. 'London has seldom been invaded by such a vast host of North Country folk,' said the *Penny Illustrated*.

Newcastle were clear favourites, despite the curse of the Palace. 'They have never had a better chance of becoming cup holders,' wrote a reporter for the *Dundee Courier*. 'Because Newcastle have been there so often and failed, some think they will never win. Barnsley will rely on a plentiful supply of force, courage and enthusiasm to see them through. Newcastle, however, also possess these desirable qualities, and added to them brains and experience, and I would rather place faith in Newcastle's brains than in Barnsley's determination. Veitch and his men have suffered disappointment in the past, but all remembrance of past failures is likely to be blotted out today.'

A short film strip exists showing scenes from the final. Colin Veitch stands on the halfway line with Barnsley captain Tommy Boyle. The film clearly shows that Veitch's black and white shirt has the Newcastle city coat of arms sewn onto the left breast – the first badge seen on a Newcastle shirt. As referee JT Ibbotson oversees the coin toss, thousands of supporters are visible in the background, packed onto the Crystal Palace bankings. Up to 80,000 fans were crammed inside, with many Newcastle fans finding vantage points in the trees that surrounded the ground. Veitch wins the coin toss, then the film abruptly cuts to him making a strong shoulder challenge on an advancing Barnsley player. There is then a brief mid-field tussle, before the film ends with the players jogging off the pitch through a tunnel of policemen.

The film, made by newsreel producers the Warwick Trading Company, was shown 'by cinematograph' at the Alhambra theatre in London on the night of the match. It's only a few minutes long, and gives more prominence to the coin toss than the actual match. That's partly because, as Mitchell and Kenyon had already demon-strated, early camera technology made it difficult to film match action, but also because, by all accounts, there wasn't a whole lot of action to film.

Underdogs Barnsley were the better team for most of the game, impressing reporters with 'long daisy-clipping passes' and 'old-time dribbling'. Much was made of the fact that only one Barnsley player earned the full wage permitted by the FA, while the Newcastle players were highly-paid internationals. Newcastle have regular-ly struggled against lower league opposition, and the same was true here. Buzzing around the field and em-barking on 'Napoleonic charges', Barnsley took the lead in the 37th minute. Wilf Bartrop surged upfield, beating Newcastle's Peter McWilliam, and drilled the ball across the goalmouth. Centre-forward George Lillycrop missed it, but Harry Tuffnell arrived to poke the ball in off the post.

Barnsley, in control of the match, were content to sit back and protect their lead. It was only in the last 15 minutes that Newcastle finally began to exert pressure. First Shepherd beat Barnsley keeper Fred Mearns, only to have his strike disallowed by the referee, with puzzled newspaper reporters presuming that it had been for offside. Then, in the 83rd minute, Jack Rutherford, 'the Newcastle Flyer', scored with a header from a Sandy Higgins free-kick. The equaliser gave Newcastle belief that the Crystal Palace curse could be broken. They pushed forward for a winner, 'with Veitch as ringleader', piling pressure onto the Barnsley defence, only to be repeatedly repelled by man of the match Dickie Downs. In the end, although Newcastle avoided defeat, they were still unable to win at the Palace. The match ended as a 1-1 draw, much to the chagrin of the large crowd.

'There was none of the hilarity that follows the ordinary cup final – none of the shouting, laughing and pushing, none of the extravagance of jubilation,' said the *Guardian*. Newcastle had failed to win again, but at least – for the first time at the Palace – they had not lost.

The disappointment of the fans was matched by that of the players. 'I prefer not to say much about the game,' said Colin Veitch. 'As things turned out we are well content to draw. It was a very hard game, and perhaps the result is as it should be. I will not commit myself to any forecast for the next match, but we certainly hope to win.'

There would need to be a tactical rethink if that was to happen. Newcastle had altered their style, specifically it seems, with a view to winning at the Palace. It hadn't quite worked. 'Known as a scientific side who play beautiful football, they have adopted more aggressive methods during the greater part of this season, with no small success,' said the *Nottingham Evening Post*, 'but when cleverness might have given them a comfortable victory they could not settle down to anything approaching effective combination.'

'It cannot be said that the play was either scientific or artistic,' commented the *Times*. 'Stoppages for minor injuries were far too frequent; it is not easy to understand why the game should be suspended by the referee merely because a large, able-bodied man is winded or gets a trifling hack. Really the cockering of the modern professional is becoming ridiculous.'

Further criticism followed when it was found that 75 'ring seats' supplied to the club for the final had been advertised for sale at almost twice their face value. The club claimed they had handed over the tickets to an unnamed player in good faith, and 'regretted the result'. The FA weren't satisfied with that explanation, and censured the club.

Some of the exhibits here in the museum are genuinely awe-inspiring. The replica Jules Rimet Trophy that was presented to Bobby Moore in 1966, after the original had been stolen, sits next to Geoff Hurst's hat-trick ball, and George Cohen's World Cup winning shirt. There's Pele's Brazil shirt from the 1958 World Cup, Bobby Moore's shirt from the 1970 game against Brazil, and Diego Maradona's 1986 'Hand of God' shirt. There are also plenty of unusual items – Tommy Lawton's ashes, Bert Trautmann's neck brace, and, less impressively, Jim White's tie from Sky Sports' transfer deadline coverage. That tie is not what I've travelled down to see.

In the aftermath of the draw, the announcement that the replay would be played on the following Thursday at Everton's Goodison Park caused some consternation among Barnsley supporters. Barnsley had beaten Everton in the semi-final, and it was thought that the Goodison crowd would favour Newcastle. Remarkably, Newcastle played two away league fixtures in the four days between the cup final and the replay. They fielded a reserve team, and beat Bristol City 3-0 on the Monday, before being thumped 0-4 by Aston Villa on the Wednesday. Then, on Thursday it was off to Goodison. 50 special trains ferried supporters from Newcastle to Liverpool.

The weather was awful, with torrential rain pouring down from early morning onwards. Despite the conditions, the ground was packed. 70,000 spectators 'turned up their coat-collars and execrated the elements wholeheartedly,' according to the *Guardian*. Half an hour before kick-off, the crowd broke through the barriers and poured onto the pitch, being pushed back by mounted police to clear the touch-lines.

The rain eventually stopped, but the pitch was saturated. 'The ground, very bare of grass except in the corners, became very slippery,' said one report. Of course, a bare and slippery Goodison Park would suit Newcastle's passing style much better than the cursed Palace.

The teams entered the field just before half-past three, to 'splendid ovations'. Barnsley's Tommy Boyle won the coin toss and allowed Newcastle to kick-off. There was just one change to the Newcastle team that had played in the first match. Full-back Tony Whitson was injured, but he was comfortably replaced by the always-dependable Jack Carr.

Barnsley started quite brightly, but their early attacks were thwarted by a brilliant McCracken, making smart interceptions and utilising his soon-to-be famed offside trap. Newcastle quickly found their feet. 'More subtle, more sure-footed, more coldly collected,' the Magpies coped better with the slippery conditions and sodden leather ball. 'No need for Newcastle to surreptitiously duck the ball in a bucket of water, as we used to do at school when we pitted our "skill" against the other side's "might",' commented the *Guardian*.

Newcastle created a series of chances – a Higgins free-kick, a Howie header, a Wilson shot that went just over the bar. Then a deflected clearance fell at the feet of the unmarked Shepherd, right in front of goal. Amazingly, though, the usually-deadly centre-forward put his shot wide. Reporters were kind to Shepherd, blaming the 'greasy ball'.

Newcastle continued to pile on the pressure, with Barnsley backs Downs and Harry Ness, along with goalkeeper Mearns, performing heroics for their side. A vicious Wilf Low free-kick was blocked by Ness, and a McWilliam shot was clawed away and cleared by Mearns. The excitement caused the crowd to spill onto the pitch, and again mounted police were required to force fans back behind the touch-lines.

In a rare exchange at the other end of the pitch, Jimmy Lawrence made an excellent full-length save from Bartrop, tipping the ball around the post. Then Newcastle resumed their offensive, with Veitch going close from a corner, Higgins having a shot blocked by Downs, and Rutherford chipping the ball narrowly over the bar. Then, in Newcastle's closest chance yet, Rutherford beat the defence, took the ball around Mearns, and rolled it towards goal, only for the keeper to somehow scramble back and push it off the goal-line and around the post. The *Guardian*'s reporter said it was 'as good a save as I have ever seen'.

At half-time, the score was still, somehow, 0-0. 'Newcastle were clearly the better side,' said one report, 'and they seemed at this point to be able to do everything but score.'

The second half started quietly, and Newcastle fans must have feared that their side would, once again, fade away in final. However, in the 52nd minute, Veitch, the game's 'star artist', started a move involving Higgins and Low that culminated with Shepherd bursting past Downs, beating the onrushing Mearns, and side-footing the ball into the back of the net. A photographer captured the moment from behind the goal, Shepherd with scissored legs in mid-air, and a teammate raising an arm in celebration. That was 1-0, and Newcastle led in a cup final for the very first time.

What followed was a frantic period of play, with peppered shots and heavy tackles, leaving both sets of players covered in mud. Higgins had a goal disallowed for offside, after chesting a Rutherford cross into the net. Then Barnsley's Downs was downed in a strong challenge, and had to be carried from the pitch 'in a semi-unconscious' condition. The Newcastle player who made the challenge doesn't seem to be named in press reports, but the *Mirror* did say, 'It was noticeable during the stoppage that other members of the Newcastle team walked away or turned their backs on the offender when he spoke to them.' Downs recovered to play on, and made some important challenges as Newcastle continued to press.

The deciding moment of the game came after Barnsley's Washington-born half-back Bob Glendenning was penalised for a foul in the area. Shepherd stepped up to take the penalty kick, driving a low shot past Mearns to make the score 2-0. Barnsley pushed for a goal that might get them back into the game, but McCracken and Carr were equal to anything that was thrown at them. On the one occasion the Newcastle backs were beaten, Lawrence made a good save from Bartrop. Eventually, though, the game came to an end. The final score was 2-0, and Newcastle had won the FA Cup.

'When the whistle went there was great cheering and hat waving, and the crowd broke over the field to get a peep at the cup,' reported the *Guardian*. 'Few grudged Newcastle their win. They have tried enough times for it, to be sure. The marvel of the game was that Newcastle won by so little as they did.'

The *Daily Express* lavished praise on the Newcastle side, starting with its 25-year-old goalkeeper. 'Not the slightest fault could be found with Lawrence, and he had more than one nasty customer to stop,' said the report. Irish international Bill McCracken had 'played brilliantly', and Jack Carr, the England international from Seaton Burn played 'such a good game'. In the middle, Veitch, Low and McWilliam were 'at the top of their form'. 'They were thoroughly sound in their tackling, and they held the Barnsley forwards completely in check, while their placing of the ball could scarcely have been better.' The *Express* said that Wilson and Higgins had combined well on the left wing, while the *Times* singled out right-sided forwards Rutherford and Howie and goalscoring hero Shepherd for praise.

The *Daily Mirror*'s match report was accompanied by two very grainy match 'photographs', wired to London 'in nine minutes' by the Thorne Baker telectrograph, a new invention that allowed the transmission of pictures over telegraph wires. It was an incredibly early version of a fax machine, and the images it produced were of similarly ropey quality. The *Mirror* withdrew its investment in the telectrograph shortly after this match. The only recognisable Newcastle player in the grainy photos is the unmistakeable figure of Colin Veitch. The *Mirror* said, 'Veitch was the star artist and his play was simply delightful.' The *Daily Telegraph* described Veitch's performance as 'outstanding'.

The team's tactics were also applauded. 'Newcastle possess men with brains, and it was easy to see that Veitch and his colleagues had weighed up their opponents,' wrote the football journalist JJ Bentley, who was also an FA and Football League committee member. The combination of the bare pitch and the wet weather had allowed Newcastle's passing style to shine. 'The cup went to the better side,' wrote Bentley, 'and while we can heartily congratulate Barnsley on the great fight they have made, we must award all praise to Newcastle United for carrying off the trophy after so many struggles. They have thoroughly earned their success.'

'There was a remarkable scene in front of the stand,' said the *Times*, as the crowd swarmed onto the pitch in order to see the presentation of the cup and medals.

Veitch received the cup from Lord Derby, and spoke a few words to the crowd. He told them that it was the proudest moment of the players' lives. The Newcastle captain was humble in victory, saying that his players knew only too well how the Barnsley men must be feeling, and what it was like to creep to their homes 'quietly and unobserved' after a defeat. He asked the crowd to show their appreciation for Barnsley's plucky fight. The defeated opponents were given 'three very hefty cheers'. Further speeches were made, 'but the cheering was so loud and prolonged that little could be heard'.

After the match, and after Newcastle's precious, long-awaited victory, the *Times* report noted that the grey skies disappeared. 'Afterwards the weather was fine; a breeze sprang up and the sun came out.'

And here, in a glass case in the museum, is the very trophy that was presented to Colin Veitch. It's only about 12 inches tall, a decorative sterling silver cup with two jug-ear handles. Perched on top of the lid is a small figure with a ball at his feet. On the front, back and sides are four plates listing the names of the FA Cup winners, starting with Wanderers in 1872. One the left-hand side, under the handle and next to the silver hallmarks, is stamped: '1910. NEWCASTLE UNITED.'

This was the second FA Cup trophy. The first was stolen in 1895, while in the possession of Aston Villa, and melted down to make counterfeit coins. This replacement, a replica of the original 'little tin idol' cup, was made by Birmingham silversmith Howard Vaughton – a former Aston Villa player. It was first awarded to The Wednesday in 1896. It was only presented 15 times, and only to 11 clubs – Wednesday twice, Aston Villa twice, Sheffield United twice, Bury twice, plus once each to Tottenham Hotspur, Nottingham Forest, Manchester City, Everton, Wolverhampton Wanderers, Manchester United and, finally, Newcastle United.

Following Newcastle's victory, the FA presented the cup as a gift to outgoing president Lord Kinnaird, who had won the original FA Cup five times as a player. For many years, the trophy was kept as an ornament on the Kinnaird family's dining table. In 2005, it was sold at auction for £478,000 to West Ham joint chairman David Gold, who then loaned it to the National Football Museum. So Newcastle were the last club to win this wonderful centenarian trophy. Geordies can think of it as our trophy, or perhaps 'wor cup'.

It would be nice to think it could be brought home to Newcastle, but its value, and the fact that Newcastle United doesn't have a club museum, makes that unlikely to happen. Still, better it is here in the excellent National Football Museum than sitting on the Kinnaird (or Gold) dining table. As nice as it would be to bring it home, I'm going to have to return to Newcastle without it.

Back in 1910, though, the victorious team did bring the FA Cup home to Newcastle, and were met at Central Station by many thousands of cheering fans. The players climbed aboard eight electric trams and, preceded by a pipe band, they moved slowly through the city centre, with Veitch and his teammates holding aloft the cup. There are some extraordinary photographs taken during the 1910 homecoming, showing thousands of men and women, in caps and bonnets, packed into Neville Street outside the Central Station portico, craning their necks and shinning up lampposts. They're parting to let through the trams, bedecked in black and white decorations. What an occasion.

Any Newcastle supporter can readily imagine what this scene must have looked like without requiring photographs. That was a city that had fallen in love with its football club, and it's a love that endures more than a hundred years later. The club still represents the people of Newcastle, and is an integral part of the city. Modern fans will recognise how the mood of the city is affected by the performance of its football team. For Newcastle United to have won something – and to have won the greatest prize that football could offer – would have lifted the hearts of its people, put a spring in their step, and made Newcastle a brighter and better place to be alive.

It had taken 30 years, but Newcastle United were now confirmed as the best football club in the country. No doubt reflecting the joyous, relieved feelings of thousands of Newcastle supporters, the *Chronicle* printed a cartoon of a magpie dancing a jig, under the headline: 'AT LAST'.

Crowds greet the Newcastle team at Central Station, 1910

Newcastle's Albert Shepherd, in rarely-seen away kit, scored twice in a 2-0 win at Oldham, 10 September 1910

12

End of an Era

The 1909/10 season saw Newcastle United reach highs that would not be matched until the 1950s. The FA Cup win, following on the back of three league championships, capped the Edwardian period as the most successful in the club's history. But the Edwardian period was coming to an end. King Edward VII died on 6 May 1910, nine days after Colin Veitch lifted the cup. It had been a successful era for Newcastle United and, in a wider sense, for the whole country, which had enjoyed relative prosperity and peace throughout Edward's reign. But there was a great war on the horizon, and things were about to change.

Certainly Newcastle's achievements had cemented the bond between the club and its city, as evidenced by the huge crowds that turned out to welcome them home. The cup win didn't necessarily attract more fans to Newcastle's matches, though. Average attendances at St James' Park remained at around 25,000, still the biggest in the country. They wouldn't reach the 50,000-plus level until after the post-Second World War football boom. But the win did rubber-stamp Newcastle's claim to be the best team in the country, and that gave the people of Newcastle something to be proud of. The great local patriotism that existed in this 'canny toon' could be channelled through support for the city's football team. That's something that continues to happen to this day.

Newcastle reached the cup final again in 1911, but were hit with a double injury blow. Already without Jimmy Howie, who had moved to Huddersfield, Newcastle lost the excellent Peter McWilliam, who was injured playing for Scotland. 'Peter the Great', still just 29, irreparably damaged his knee ligaments, and never played football again. He did go on to become a successful manager, however, with Spurs and Middlesbrough.

Then, just a week before the final against fellow first division side Bradford City, Albert Shepherd was badly injured in a collision with Blackburn goalkeeper Jimmy Ashcroft. Shepherd had scored 33 goals in the 1910/11 season. He'd also made his long-awaited second appearance for England, and scored a second international goal. Two games and two goals, but he never played for his country again. It was another knee ligament injury, and, although Shepherd would eventually return to football after an 18-month absence, he would never be the same player.

In Shepherd's absence, Newcastle looked for goals from Jimmy 'Tadger' Stewart. The Gateshead-born England international had scored 13 that season, including one in the semi-final against Chelsea. Tadger Stewart's 1911 cup final shirt is on display at the National Football Museum, in the same glass case as the 1910 FA Cup. It's a wonderful item – a heavy long-sleeved shirt with broad black and white stripes and a laced collar. On the right breast is a wonderfully-detailed embroidered badge featuring the city crest.

Stewart didn't score in the 1911 final – in fact no one did. Veitch was typically outstanding, but Newcastle failed to win at the Crystal Palace once again as the game ended 0-0. The replay was at the recently-opened Old Trafford. Away from their bogey ground, Newcastle were expected to win, although Bradford had beaten them in the league just a few weeks earlier. Calamity struck after quarter of an hour. A clash in the Newcastle penalty area left Bradford's Frank Thompson severely bloodied and Newcastle's Jimmy Lawrence severely distracted. But play continued, and Frank O'Rourke headed into the unguarded net. Veitch came close to grabbing an equaliser with a couple of dangerous long range shots, but Bradford held out to win. They were presented with the new FA Cup trophy, a version of which is still in use today. Newcastle had played in seven FA Cup final matches, including replays, between 1905 and 1911, and had won only one of them.

As the Great War approached, Newcastle's team of great masters came apart. Jack Carr retired from playing and became an assistant trainer. He later became the manager of Blackburn Rovers. Jack Rutherford was transferred to Arsenal in 1913, and Sandy Higgins moved to Kilmarnock. The careers of George Wilson and others were effectively ended by the war. Only McCracken, Jimmy Lawrence and Wilf Low would still be at the club once football resumed in 1919.

As for Colin Veitch, despite a major falling out with

the club's directors, presumably because they didn't agree with his firm views on how the team should be run, he continued to play for Newcastle up until the war. But he became less influential, and was replaced as club captain by Bill McCracken.

Away from football, Veitch continued his passion for music and theatre. He had been a member of the Newcastle Operatic Society and Clarion Choir throughout his football career, and in 1911 he co-founded the Clarion Dramatic Society, which was affiliated to the socialist movement. The society, which would soon change its name to the People's Theatre, was based not far from St James' Park on Percy Street (in a building that now houses a joke shop). Veitch remained an active member of the Theatre for most of the remainder of his life. The People's Theatre still exists, and, since 1962, has been based in its well-known building in Heaton, at the Newcastle end of the Coast Road, next to the Corner House pub.

In 1914 Veitch appeared in *The Musical Herald* (a kind of Edwardian *NME*). 'The socialists seek to put an end to competition, but apparently this does not apply to music,' the paper wrote. The Newcastle Clarion Choir had won a contest held at the Free Trade Hall in Manchester. *The Music Herald* reported that they were, 'conducted by Mr Colin Veitch, a well-known member of the Newcastle United Football Team.'

Veitch made his last appearance for Newcastle in September 1914, aged 33, and was then sent to war. Conscripted into the Army, he reached the rank of 2nd Lieutenant. After the war, Veitch returned to Newcastle United to take up a coaching post. He also opened a newsagents on Shields Road in Byker, but this was closed after the sudden early death of his wife Minnie. He subsequently married a People's Theatre actress named Greta Burke, who was famous across Tyneside. The celebrity couple were a big draw in and around theatre circles. They acted together on stage and in radio dramas – and also in more unusual settings. They were said to perform the balcony scene from *Romeo and Juliet* outside their house for the benefit of their neighbours.

Veitch continued to be active politically, although his People's Theatre abandoned its links with the socialist movement. He was twice approached by the Labour Party to run for Parliament, but turned down the opportunity to become an MP.

Despite his wide interests, Veitch never strayed too far from football. In 1923 he helped to re-establish the Newcastle United Swifts, a nursery team for developing youth players. This looked like a valuable contribution to the black and white cause, but, in 1926, the Swifts were disbanded and Veitch's coaching contract with the club was terminated. His 27 years at Newcastle United were at an end.

After a brief and fairly unsuccessful spell in management at Bradford City – the club that had prevented him from lifting the cup in 1911 – Veitch returned to Newcastle, and began to write about football and other sports for the *Evening Chronicle* and *Sunday Sun*. He also got into broadcasting, and worked as an early football pundit, reviewing matches for regional BBC radio programmes.

Interestingly, one of Veitch's journalistic tasks was

to write an obituary for the great Frank Watt, who died in 1932, aged 77. In his *Sunday Sun* column, Colin Veitch wrote, 'It is no exaggeration to state that the great edifice known as Newcastle United was built around Frank Watt – and, largely, by him.'

Then, in July 1938, Veitch fell ill, and took a trip to Switzerland to recuperate. While there he contracted pneumonia. Colin Veitch died in a hospital in Berne on 26 August 1938. He was 57 years old.

After Veitch's death, William Pickford the president of the FA said, 'I could not speak more highly of him, and his death is a great loss to football. He was a player of the highest type both in his standard of playing and his conduct and a fine example to others. I always held him in the highest regard. He was one of the best half-backs football has produced and an inspiration to Newcastle during their greatest days.'

The Times said Veitch had been 'one of the finest footballers in the country'. The *Chronicle* described him, using a memorable phrase, as 'a man of striking parts'.

Colin Veitch hasn't been forgotten on Tyneside. In 2012 he came fourth in the *Chronicle*'s '100 Greatest Geordies' poll, behind Catherine Cookson, Bobby Robson and winner Jackie Milburn, and ahead of fifth-placed Alan Shearer. In 2013, a plaque was unveiled outside his former home at 1 Stratford Villas in Newcastle. 'Colin Veitch, 1881-1938,' says the plaque. 'Captain of Newcastle United FC during their trophy-winning Edwardian heyday. Co-founder of the People's Theatre and the Professional Footballer's Association. Sportsman, actor, politician.' Above all else, he had played a striking part in making Newcastle United great.

He wasn't the only one, of course. It had all begun back at Stanley Street with William Coulson, John Armstrong and friends. Then in Byker and Heaton there had been Alec White and James Miller, and the great manager Tom Watson. Importantly, there were those early fans, who had supported the club in voice ('Play up, East End!') and in cash. The move to St James' and the name change to United alienated some of those fans, but they came back on board to watch the likes of Willie Thompson and Jock Peddie fire the club into the Football League, and to promotion to the first division.

Then came Andy Aitken and Bob McColl, and the brilliant leadership of Frank Watt. Now Newcastle United truly became great, challenging for and winning the league championship, with players like Jack Rutherford, Alec Gardner and Bill Appleyard. There were more fans now, at least 25,000 at every match, sometimes nearer 60,000, and hundreds of thousands turning up to welcome the players home when the won the league for a second and third time. And there were more great players – Jimmy Lawrence, Bill McCracken and that man Veitch. And Albert Shepherd, who fired the club to its greatest triumph – the long-awaited FA Cup win.

The first 30 years of Newcastle United were formative for the club, its supporters and the city. It was a period during which our ancestors built and fell in love with Newcastle United Football Club, and in doing so they helped to shape who we are today. It's said that you have to know the past to understand the present. Exploring Newcastle United's past helps to explain why the club continues to mean so much to so many. Newcastle's wonderful history is something to be proud of. It's the foundation on which the club's future is built, and we can only hope for more great days ahead. *Howay the lads.*

St James' Park in an aerial photograph of Newcastle upon Tyne, taken by United fan and windscreen wiper inventor Gladstone Adams, September 1917 (courtesy Tyne & Wear Archives)

Acknowledgements

When setting out to write a football history book you must inevitably travel down paths that have already been trodden, particularly when studying such a popular subject as Newcastle United. You can only hope to walk those paths in different ways, and perhaps stumble across things that have not already been stumbled upon. In particular, these paths have been well-trodden by the official club historian Paul Joannou, and previously by the journalist Arthur Appleton, whose authoritative books on the subject are listed in the bibliography. I doff my flat cap to them, and to the other referenced authors.

The majority of sources for this book were found in newspaper archives, and I am indebted to those who have catalogued and maintained these archives, and to our valuable public libraries. Thanks to my mam, Carol Brown, for providing family history research! Thanks also to Paul J White, who helped me locate and photograph the club's early grounds.

Final thanks go to everyone who has supported the book through its writing and publication, and particularly to Louise for her patience and encouragement.

Selected Bibliography

Books

Association Football & The Men Who Made It, Alfred Gibson & William Pickford (Caxton, 1906)

The Book of Football, JH Morrison et al (Amalgamated, 1905-06)

A Complete Who's Who of Newcastle United, Paul Joannou (Newcastle United Supporters' Club, 1983)

A Day in Newcastle, Frederick Gosman (A Reid, 1878)

Football League: Grounds for a Change, Dave Twydell (Yore Publications, 1991)

Football Through The Turnstiles... Again, Brian Tabner (Yore Publications, 2002)

Hotbed of Soccer, Arthur Appleton (Hart-Davis, 1960)

Newcastle United: The Ultimate Record, Paul Joannou with Alan Candlish & Bill Swann (N Publishing, 2011)

The North-East Ports, William Clark Russell (A Reid, 1883)

Northern Goalfields, Brian Hunt (York, 1989)

Pioneers of the North, Paul Joannou & Alan Candlish (Breedon Books, 2009)

Ward's Directory of Newcastle-on-Tyne (Ward & Sons, 1890s)

Wickets and Goals, JAH Catton (Chapman & Hall, 1926)

Articles

Out With a League Team, Henry Leach (*Chums*, March 1900)

Football of Yesterday and Today, Harold McFarlane (*The Monthly Review*, October 1906)

The New Football Mania, Charles Edwards (*The Nineteenth Century*, October 1892)

Who Invested in Victorian Football Clubs?, Neal Garnham & Andrew Jackson (*Soccer & Society*, 4:1, 2003)

Newspapers

Athletic News

Bell's Life in London and Sporting Chronicle

Daily Express

Daily Mirror

Daily News

The Graphic

The Guardian

Kentish Independent

London Standard

Morpeth Herald

Newcastle Daily Chronicle

Newcastle Daily Journal

Newcastle Courant

Northern Echo

Penny Illustrated

Sheffield Evening Telegraph

Sunderland Daily Echo

The Telegraph

The Times

Tyneside Daily Echo

Websites

11v11.com (www.11v11.com)

Historical Football Kits (www.historicalkits.co.uk)

Statto.com (www.statto.com)

They Wore the Newcastle Shirt
(www.nufctheyworethenewcastleshirt.btck.co.uk)

Vision of Britain; Census Reports
(www.visionofbritain.org.uk/census)

Videos

Newcastle United v Liverpool, 1901 (Mitchell & Kenyon,
www.bit.ly/1jyzhBY)

Everton v Newcastle United, 1902 (Mitchell & Kenyon,
www.bit.ly/1qs8Oxv)

Newcastle United v Barnsley, 1910 Cup Final (Warwick,
www.youtube.com/watch?v=jf5tTyhMjBk)

Newcastle United v Bradford City, 1911 Cup Final (Warwick, www.bit.ly/1nPlI5e)

Newcastle United v Bradford City, 1911 Cup Final Replay
(Unknown, www.bit.ly/1so8cKZ)

Index

About the Author

Paul Brown is a freelance writer and Newcastle United season ticket holder. He has written about Newcastle and football history for publications including *The Guardian, FourFourTwo, When Saturday Comes* and *The Blizzard*. He is the author of six books including *The Victorian Football Miscellany, Unofficial Football World Champions* and *Black and White Army: A Season Supporting Newcastle United*.

Website:
www.stuffbypaulbrown.com

Twitter:
@paulbrownUK

Also Available

The Victorian Football Miscellany

A collection of interesting, amusing and eye-opening stories, facts and statistics from the earliest days of football.

'One of the greatest books ever written about football since Charlie Buchan put down his pen!' – Danny Baker

'Hugely entertaining.' – *When Saturday Comes*

In paperback and on Kindle

Unofficial Football World Champions

Tracing football's alternative 'winner-stays-on' championships from the very first international match in 1872, right up to 2014.

'A fascinating history of football. *****' – *FourFourTwo*

In paperback and on Kindle

Black & White Army: A Season Supporting Newcastle United

Following Newcastle supporters through the 2002/03 Champions League season, one of the most memorable seasons in recent memory. Specially-updated tenth anniversary eBook edition, with proceeds going to the Sir Bobby Robson Foundation.

On Kindle and iPad

Lightning Source UK Ltd.
Milton Keynes UK
UKOW05f0916291116
288789UK00010B/121/P